All-in-One Bible Fun
Fruit of the Spirit
Preschool

Also available from Abingdon Press

All-in-One Bible Fun

Fruit of the Spirit
Elementary

Stories of Jesus
Preschool

Stories of Jesus
Elementary

Favorite Bible Stories
Preschool

Favorite Bible Stories
Elementary

Heroes of the Bible
Preschool

Heroes of the Bible
Elementary

Writer/Editor: Daphna Flegal
Production Editors: Billie Brownell, Anna Raitt
Production and Design Manager: Marcia C'deBaca
Illustrator: Robert S. Jones
Cover images: jupiterimages

All-in-One

BIBLE

FUN

Fruit of the Spirit
Preschool

ABINGDON PRESS
Nashville

All-in-One Bible Fun
Fruit of the Spirit
Preschool

ISBN 9781426707858

09 10 11 12 13 14 15 16 17 18 - 10 9 8 7 6 5 4 3 2 1

MANUFACTURED IN THE UNITED STATES OF AMERICA

All-in-One BIBLE FUN Table of Contents

Bible Units in *Fruit of the Spirit*

Use these combinations if you choose to organize the lessons in short-term units.

Fruit of the Spirit

Bible Story	Bible Verse
Love	Love is kind. 1 Corinthians 13:4
Joy	Sing for joy to the LORD, all the earth. Psalm 98:4, GNT
Peace	Happy are those who work for peace. Matthew 5:9, GNT
Patience	Be patient and wait for the LORD to act. Psalm 37:7, GNT
Kindness	Be kind to one another. Ephesians 4:32
Generosity	God loves a cheerful giver. 2 Corinthians 9:7
Faithfulness	Be faithful to God. Joshua 22:5, GNT, adapted
Gentleness	Let your gentleness be known to everyone. Philippians 4:5
Self-control	Let us choose what is right. Job 34:4

Other Christian Virtues

Bible Story	Bible Verse
Honesty	Be honest. Proverbs 14:2, GNT
Forgiveness	Forgive one another. Ephesians 4:32, GNT
Obedience	Children, obey your parents. Ephesians 6:1
Responsibility	Do good to everyone. Galatians 6:10, GNT

Supplies

(This is a comprehensive list of all the supplies needed if you choose to do all the activities. It is your choice whether your group will do all the activities.)

- Bible
- construction paper
- plain paper
- glue
- safety scissors, scissors
- clear tape
- masking tape
- stapler, staples
- crayons, watercolor markers, scented markers
- newspaper
- paper plates
- paper cups
- plastic or real coins
- clean coffee can or other metal container
- small paper bags
- paper towels
- tempera paint, paintbrushes
- shallow trays or box lids
- paint smocks
- drinking straws
- paper punch
- ribbon or crepe paper

- yarn or string
- baskets or boxes
- ball
- drum, rhythm instruments, blocks, or unsharpened pencils
- chairs
- mural paper (such as bulletin board paper)
- large bowl or plastic tub
- flour, salt, water
- plastic squeeze bottles
- white feathers
- play dough or clay
- towel or cloth
- trash can
- dishwashing liquid
- envelopes
- colored tissue paper
- pennies or metal washers
- chenille stems
- sandpaper or corrugated cardboard
- heart stickers, happy face stickers
- plastic fruit
- CD of Christian music and CD player
- handwashing supplies

Welcome to
All-in-One Bible Fun

Have fun learning about the fruit of the Spirit! Each lesson in this teacher guide is filled with games and activities that will make learning fun for you and your children. Everything you need to teach is included in Abingdon's *All-in-One Bible Fun*, and with just a few additional supplies, your group can enjoy fun and enriching activities. Each lesson also has a box with a picture of a cookie,

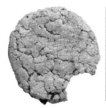

> # We celebrate with joy because we know Jesus is alive!

that is repeated over and over again throughout the lesson. The cookie box states the Bible message in words your children will understand.

Use the following tips to help make *All-in-One Bible Fun* a success!

- Read through each lesson. Read the Bible passages.

- Memorize the Bible verse and the cookie box statement.

- Choose activities that fit your unique group of children and your time limitations. If time is limited, those activities we recommend are in **boldface** on the chart page and noted by a *balloon* beside each activity.

balloon symbol

- Practice telling the Bible story.

- Gather the supplies you will use for the lesson.

- Learn the music included in each lesson. All the songs are written to familiar tunes.

- Arrange your room space to fit the lesson. Move tables and chairs so there is plenty of room for the children to move and to sit on the floor.

- Copy the Reproducible pages for the lesson.

Preschoolers

Each child in your class is a one-of-a-kind child of God. Each child has his or her own name, background, family situation, and set of experiences. It is important to remember and celebrate the uniqueness of each child. Yet all of these one-of-a-kind children of God have some common needs.

- All children need love.
- All children need a sense of self-worth.
- All children need to feel a sense of accomplishment.
- All children need to have a safe place to be and to express their feelings.
- All children need to be surrounded by adults who love them.
- All children need to experience the love of God.

Preschoolers (children 3–5 years old) also have some common characteristics.

Their Bodies

- They do not sit still for very long.
- They have lots of energy.
- They enjoy moving (running, galloping, dancing, jumping, hopping).
- They are developing fine motor skills (learning to cut with scissors, learning to handle a ball, learning to tie their shoes).
- They enjoy using their senses (taste, touch, smell, hearing, seeing).

Their Minds

- They are learning more and more words.
- They enjoy music.
- They are learning to express their feelings.
- They like to laugh and be silly.
- They enjoy nonsense words.
- They are learning to identify colors, sizes, and shapes.
- They have an unclear understanding of time.
- They have a wonderful imagination.

Their Relationships

- They are beginning to interact with others as they play together.
- They are beginning to understand that other people have feelings.
- They are learning to wait for their turn.
- They can have a hard time leaving parents, especially their mother.
- They want to help.
- They love to feel important.

Their Hearts

- They need to handle the Bible and see others handle it.
- They need caring adults who model Christian attitudes and behaviors.
- They need to sing, move to, and say Bible verses.
- They need to hear clear, simple stories from the Bible.
- They can express simple prayers.
- They can experience wonder and awe at God's world.
- They can share food and money and make things for others.
- They can experience belonging at church.

All-in-One

BIBLE PRESCHOOL

FUN

Love

Bible Verse

Love is kind.

1 Corinthians 13:4

Bible Story

Galatians 5:22–23; 1 Corinthians 13

The term "fruit of the Spirit" comes from the idea that Christians grow in the faith, and this growth produces Christian virtues such as love and joy. The fruit of love is self-giving love. It is generous and unconditional. It is the kind of love God offers each one of us.

The Bible story for today comes from one of Paul's most famous letters. Paul is credited with writing over 25 percent of the New Testament. Paul's letters were an important part of his ministry. Whether he was in prison or just in another part of the world, Paul used his letters to communicate with other members of the early church.

The form of Paul's letters makes it obvious that he intended for them to be read aloud to the individual congregations. Through his letters Paul taught the churches. The letters begin with a salutation, continue with

the reason for the letter, and close with a benediction. He criticized the churches, corrected them, praised them, or pleaded with them, depending on what was needed at the time.

Children love to get mail. This week is a perfect opportunity to send your children a card or letter. You may use the heart on page 19 to make cards to send to your children. Send it the week before or the week after the lesson; either is timely.

In this letter Paul dwells on the qualities of love. Throughout the Gospels Jesus calls his followers to love one another. Help the children see that they one way they can show love is by being kind.

We can show love to others.

If time is limited, we recommend those activities that are noted in **boldface**. Depending on your time and the number of children, you may be able to include more activities.

ACTIVITY	TIME	SUPPLIES
Fruit Fun	**5 minutes**	**Reproducible 1A, scissors**
Great Garlands	10 minutes	Reproducible 1A, scissors and safety scissors, paper punch, crayons or markers, yarn, drinking straws, tape
Heartshake	15 minutes	2 thin paper plates per child, crayons or markers, tape, crepe paper or ribbon, scissors, optional: heart stickers
Bible Story: A Love Letter	**10 minutes**	**None**
Bible Verse Fun	**5 minutes**	**Bible**
Fruit Frolic	10 minutes	plastic fruit or Reproducible 1A
Love Letters	10 minutes	Reproducible 1B, scissors, markers or crayons, ribbon or yarn, optional: paper cutter
Fruit Roll-ups	5 minutes	ball
Fruit of the Spirit Prayers	**5 minutes**	**None**

JOIN THE FUN

BIBLE STORY FUN

LIVE THE FUN

Supplies

Reproducible
1A, scissors

Fruit Fun

Photocopy and cut apart at least two sets of the fruit pictures (**Reproducible 1A**). Mix up the pictures and place them on a table or rug. Let the children enjoy matching the pictures.

Ask: What do you see in these pictures? (*fruit*)

Say: These fruits are called the fruit of the Spirit. A man named Paul wrote a letter to his friends about how we grow when we learn about Jesus. "We are like a tree that grows fruit," wrote Paul. "But our fruit is not the kind of fruit we eat. It is not apples and bananas and grapes. The fruit of the Spirit is love, joy, peace, patience, kindness, generosity, faithfulness, gentleness, and self-control." Love is one of the fruit of the Spirit. God's Spirit gives us love to help us live the way God wants us to live. Our Bible story today is about a man named Paul who wrote a letter to tell his friends about love. Paul said love is kind. When we are kind to others, we are showing love.

> **We can show love to others.**

Supplies

Reproducible
1A, scissors
and safety
scissors, paper
punch,
crayons or
markers, yarn,
drinking
straws, tape

Great Garlands

Photocopy and cut apart several copies of the fruit pictures (**Reproducible 1A**). Use a paper punch to punch a hole in the top of each picture. Let the children decorate the pictures with crayons or markers.

Cut yarn into 18-inch lengths. Give the children several drinking straws. Show the children how to cut the drinking straws into smaller pieces using safety scissors.

Then show the children how to string the straws and the fruit pictures onto the yarn. If you wrap one end of the yarn with tape, it will be easier to string the straw pieces and fruit pictures together.

When the children have finished, tie each length of yarn together to make a garland. Hang the garland in your room.

Say: The fruit pictures can help us remember that love is a fruit of the Spirit. When we are kind to others we are showing love.

Heartshake

You will need two thin paper plates (the inexpensive kind) for each child.

Have the children decorate the bottoms of each plate with crayons or markers. Let the children add heart stickers if you have provided them. Help the children fold each paper plate in half so that the decorated side faces out.

Cut brightly colored crepe paper streamers or ribbon into 24-inch lengths. Then have each child select eight streamers (four for each shaker). Tape together the ends of each group of four. Then tape a set of streamers to the inside of each of the folded paper plates.

Tape the sides of each plate together, leaving one edge open. Show the children how to slip their hands inside the openings.

Say: Love is one of the fruit of the Spirit. Our Bible story today is a letter that tells us about love.

Have the children bring their heartshakers and move to an open area of the room. Say the following action poem and do the motions with the children.

Supplies

2 thin paper plates per child, crayons or markers, tape, crepe paper or ribbon, scissors, optional: heart stickers

Shake, shake, shake,
(Shake heartshaker.)
Shake, shake, shake.
(Shake heartshaker.)
Shake it up high;
(Hold heartshaker up high.)
Shake it down low.
(Hold heartshaker low.)
Shake, shake, shake.
(Shake heartshaker.)

A fruit of the Spirit is love.
(Hold heartshaker over heart.)
Let's shake, shake, shake for love.
(Shake heartshaker.)
Shake it up high;
(Hold heartshaker up high.)
Shake it down low.
(Hold heartshaker low.)
Shake, shake, shake, for love.
(Shake heartshaker.)

Shake, shake, shake,
(Shake heartshaker.)
Shake, shake, shake.
(Shake heartshaker.)
Shake it up high;
(Hold heartshaker up high.)
Shake it down low.
(Hold heartshaker low.)
Shake, shake, shake.
(Shake heartshaker.)

A Love Letter

by Sharilyn S. Adair

Have the children sit down in your story area.
Say: *A man named Paul wrote a letter to a church. He told the people in the church all about love. His letter is in the Bible. I will tell you some things Paul said about love; then I will ask about some actions. If the actions do not show love, stamp your feet up and down, and say, "No! No! No!" If the actions do show love, clap your hands and say, "Yes! Yes! Yes!"*

Love is patient.
(Clap hands and say, "Yes! Yes! Yes!")

Is love taking someone else's turn? *(Stamp feet and say, "No! No! No!")*

No, no! Love is patient. Love can wait. Love is happy for other people to have a turn.

Love is kind.
(Clap hands and say, "Yes! Yes! Yes!")

Is love pushing and shoving on the playground? *(Stamp feet and say, "No! No! No!")*

No, no! Love is kind. Love does not hurt anyone else or make anyone else feel bad.

Love is not jealous; love does not want what others have.
(Clap hands and say, "Yes! Yes! Yes!")

Is love crying because I want *(name child in class)*'s bear? *(Stamp feet and say, "No! No! No!")*

No, no! Love is glad for others to have nice things. Love is thankful for my own things.

Love is not bragging; love does not think it is better than others.
(Clap hands and say, "Yes! Yes! Yes!")

Is love being glad that I am taller or can run faster than another child? *(Stamp feet and say, "No! No! No!")*

No, no! Love wants everyone to be happy.

Love is not selfish.
(Clap hands and say, "Yes! Yes! Yes!")

Is love showing off my new toys and not letting others play with them? *(Stamp feet and say, "No! No! No!")*

No, no! Love is sharing. Love wants everyone to have some.

Love does not have to have its own way.
(Clap hands and say, "Yes! Yes! Yes!")

Is love crying in the grocery store because Mother won't buy the cereal I want? *(Stamp feet and say, "No! No! No!")*

No, no! Love listens to others. Love knows that parents usually know what's best.

Love is happy about telling the truth.
(Clap hands and say, "Yes! Yes! Yes!")

Is love saying someone else spilled the milk when I was the one? *(Stamp feet and say, "No! No! No!")*

No, no! Love never tells a lie.

Love never ends.
(Clap hands and say, "Yes! Yes! Yes!")

God will always love us.
(Clap hands and say, "Yes! Yes! Yes!")

Bible Verse Fun

Choose a child to hold the Bible open to 1 Corinthians 13:4.

Say: Love is one of the fruit of the Spirit. Today our Bible story is the letter Paul wrote about love. Paul wrote that love is kind. He wanted people to know that God wants us to show love to others by being kind.

We can show love to others.

Say the Bible verse, "Love is kind" (1 Corinthians 3:4), for the children. Have the children say the Bible verse after you.

Help the children learn the Bible verse by singing. Sing the words printed below to the tune of "Row, Row, Row Your Boat."

> Love, love, love is kind.
> Love is kind, you see.
> The Bible tells us love is kind.
> Now sing again with me.
> © 1997 Abingdon Press.

Let the children move to the Bible verse. Have the children stand in an open area of the room. Say the statements printed below and do the suggested motions with the children. Encourage the children to repeat the Bible verse "Love is kind" (1 Corinthians 13:4) with you.

We show love when we smile at our friends. Everybody smile. *(Point to mouth and smile.)*

Love is kind.

We show love when we help pick up our toys. Let's pick up our toys. *(Pretend to pick up toys from the floor.)*

Love is kind.

We show love when we are quiet so our baby sisters can sleep. Let's tiptoe past the baby. *(Tiptoe in place; put finger over lips.)*

Love is kind.

We show love when we give our moms or dads a hug. Let's give a hug. *(Hug yourself.)*

Love is kind.

We show love when we call our grandparents on the telephone and say, "I love you!" Let's talk on the phone. *(Pretend to talk on telephone.)*

Love is kind.

We show love when we help at home. Let's pretend to sweep the floor. *(Pretend to sweep the floor.)*

Love is kind.

Fruit Frolic

Supplies

plastic fruit or Reproducible 1A

Have the children stand in a line on one side of the room. Show the children the plastic fruit like an apple or banana. If you don't have a plastic fruit use one of the pictures from **Reproducible 1A**.

Say: **Jesus taught us how to live the way God wants us to live. God wants us to live with love. Love is one of the fruit of the Spirit. Our Bible story today is about a letter a man named Paul wrote to tell his friends about love.**

Place the fruit on the floor or on a chair across the room. Choose the first child in line to begin the game.

Say: *(Child's name)*, **hop to the fruit and be kind.**

Have the child hop across the room and pick up the fruit. Have the child hold the fruit and repeat the Bible verse, "Love is kind" (1 Corinthians 13:4). Then have the child place the fruit back on the floor or chair and run back to the end of the line.

Repeat the game with each child. Vary how you tell each child to move *(tip-toe, walk backwards, jump, crawl, take giant steps, take baby steps, and so forth).*

Love Letters

Supplies

Reproducible 1B, scissors, markers or crayons, ribbon or yarn, optional: paper cutter

Photocopy several copies of the heart card **(Reproducible 1B)** for each child. If you have one, use a paper cutter to cut off the bottom of each page along the solid line.

Give each child several cards. Let the children decorate their cards with crayons or markers. Show the children how to fold the note cards along the dotted lines. Tie each child's folded note cards together with ribbon or yarn.

Say: **Today our Bible story is the letter Paul wrote about love. Paul wrote that love is kind. He wanted people to know that when we are kind to others we are showing love.**

We can show love to others.

Say: **You can give your note cards to a friend of someone in your family to help that person remember that love is kind.**

If you choose to have each child make only one note card, keep the card and send the card to the child during the week.

Fruit Roll-ups

Have the children sit in a circle with their legs spread apart.

Say: A man named Paul wrote a letter to his friends about how we grow when we learn about Jesus. "We are like a tree that grows fruit," wrote Paul. "But our fruit is not the kind of fruit we eat. It is not apples and bananas and grapes. The fruit of the Spirit is love, joy, peace, patience, kindness, generosity, faithfulness, gentleness, and self-control." Today we are learning about love.

(*Child's name*), God's Spirit gives you love.

Roll the ball to the child you named. Have the child repeat the word *love* and then roll the ball back to you. Continue around the circle until each child has a turn saying the word and rolling the ball.

Fruit of the Spirit Prayers

Have the children stand in a circle.

Say: Love is one of the fruit of the Spirit. Paul wrote a letter to tell his friends that "Love is kind." When we are kind to others we are showing love. Listen to a poem that about the fruit of the Spirit. Say the words of the poem after me and do what I do.

Love, joy, peace
are words that show we care.
So give a hug, (*Hug yourself.*)
laugh out loud, (*Put your hands on your stomach and shake.*)
then say a quiet prayer. (*Fold hands in prayer.*)

Patience, kindness, generosity
remind us what to do.
Wait for our turn, (*Stand still.*)
act with love, (*Point to your heart.*)
and share with others too. (*Move arms out as if presenting a gift.*)

Faithfulness, gentleness, self-control
are three big words to know.
Trust our great God, (*Cross your hands over your heart.*)
use kind words, (*Cup hands around mouth.*)
and choose right as we grow. (*Squat down and then stretch up tall.*)

Pray: Thank you, God, for all the ways we can show love to others. Thank you for always loving us. Amen.

Love

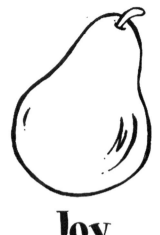

Joy

Peace

Patience

Kindness

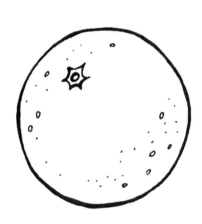

Generosity

Faithfulness

Gentleness

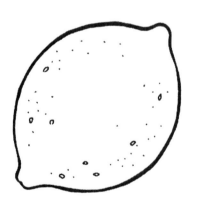

Self-control

REPRODUCIBLE 1A

Note: This page may be used in several lessons.

ALL–IN–ONE BIBLE FUN

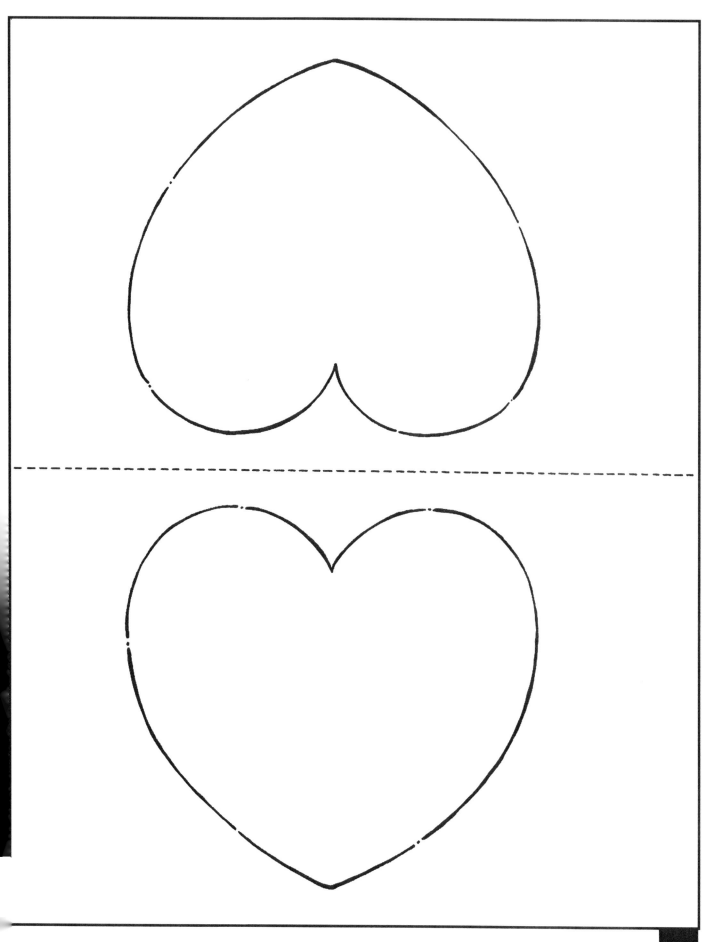

REPRODUCIBLE 1B

Joy

Bible Verse

Sing for joy to the LORD, all the earth.

Psalm 98:4, GNT

Bible Story

Galatians 5:22–23; Matthew 28:1–10

Joy is the second fruit of the Spirit listed in Galatians 5:22–23. Often we mistake joy for happiness, but happiness usually is the result of something that happens to us. For example, going on a vacation makes us happy. But joy is not a response to what happens to us. Joy is a response to God's self-giving love and care for each of us. Joy is the gladness we feel because of our redemption through Christ.

We are called to be joyful because of Christ. JESUS LIVES! The hope of Christianity is centered on this joyous event.

In Matthew's Gospel account of the resurrection, Mary Magdalene and the other Mary went to the tomb. Upon arriving at the tomb they found an angel of the Lord. The angel told them that they would not find Jesus there, for he had been raised from the dead. He then told them to go and tell the disciples. The women ran "with fear and great joy" (Matthew 28:8) to tell the disci-

ples what had happened when they met Jesus himself! When something this exciting and this joyful happens, it is impossible not to tell everyone you meet.

Jesus' resurrection assures us that God does triumph over all. It shows us that sinful separation from God and death is not all there is for us, but that God brings life out of death! Hope lives, and that hope is for us. This joyful resurrection experience shapes our lives in powerful new ways—ways we will want to tell others about. It's such good news!

Preschool children may not be able to fully understand the joy we talk about when we talk about Jesus' resurrection. What happened that day was without precedent—then or now. But children experience joy. Help them relate this joy to an even greater sense of joy that they will grow into as Christians.

We celebrate with joy because we know Jesus is alive!

If time is limited, we recommend those activities that are noted in **boldface**. Depending on your time and the number of children, you may be able to include more activities.

ACTIVITY	TIME	SUPPLIES	
Fruit Fun	**5 minutes**	**Reproducible 1A, scissors**	JOIN THE FUN
Celebration Stations	10 minutes	Reproducible 2A; scissors; masking tape, string, or construction paper; four chairs	
Shake 'n Celebrate	5 minutes	None	BIBLE STORY FUN
Bible Story: Sing for Joy	**10 minutes**	**None**	
Bible Verse Fun	**5 minutes**	**Bible**	
All the Earth	10 minutes	Reproducible 2B, crayons, thinned blue tempera paint, plastic containers, paintbrushes, newspaper, smocks	
Joy Jiggles	10 minutes	mural paper or tablecloth paper, watercolor markers, tape, optional: CD of Christian music, CD player	
Fruit Roll-ups	5 minutes	ball	LIVE THE FUN
Fruit of the Spirit Prayers	**5 minutes**	**None**	

JOIN THE FUN

Supplies

Reproducible
1A, scissors

Fruit Fun

Photocopy and cut apart at least two sets of the fruit pictures from Lesson 1 (**Reproducible 1A, page 18**). Mix up the pictures and place them on a table or rug. Let the children enjoy matching the pictures.

Ask: What do you see in these pictures? *(fruit)*

Say: These fruits are called the fruit of the Spirit. A man named Paul wrote a letter to his friends about how we grow when we learn about Jesus. "We are like a tree that grows fruit," wrote Paul. "But our fruit is not the kind of fruit we eat. It is not apples and bananas and grapes. The fruit of the Spirit is love, joy, peace, patience, kindness, generosity, faithfulness, gentleness, and self-control." Joy is one of the fruit of the Spirit. God's Spirit gives us joy to help us live the way God wants us to live. Our Bible story today is about the joy Jesus' friends felt when they knew Jesus was alive.

> **We celebrate with joy because we know Jesus is alive!**

Supplies

Reproducible
2A; scissors;
masking tape,
string, or con-
struction
paper; four
chairs

Celebration Stations

Photocopy and cut apart the movement cards (**Reproducible 2A**). Use string, masking tape, or construction paper footprints to mark a path around the floor of your room. At intervals along the path place four chairs. Tape one of the movement cards on each chair.

Tell the children to follow the path, to stop at each chair, and to do what the sign shows. Demonstrate for the children if they seem uncertain about what to do. Have the children go through the path several times. Encourage the children to move through the path slowly, and then to move through the path again quickly.

Say: Joy is one of the fruit of the Spirit. Our Bible story today is about the joy Jesus' friends felt when they knew Jesus was alive.

> **We celebrate with joy because we know Jesus is alive!**

Shake 'n Celebrate

Say: Joy is one of the fruit of the Spirit. Our Bible story today is about the joy Jesus' friends felt when they knew Jesus was alive.

> ## We celebrate with joy because we know Jesus is alive!

Have the children move to an open area of the room. Say the following action poem and do the motions with the children.

Shake, shake, shake,
(Shake hands in front of your body.)
Shake, shake, shake.
(Shake hands in front of your body.)
Shake it up high;
(Shake hands up high over your head.)
Shake it down low.
(Shake hands down low beside your knees.)
Shake, shake, shake.
(Shake hands in front of your body.)

A fruit of the Spirit is joy.
(Place hands over your heart.)
Let's shake, shake, shake for joy.
(Shake hands in front of your body.)
Shake it up high;
(Shake hands up high over your head.)
Shake it down low.
(Shake hands down low beside your knees.)
Shake, shake, shake for joy.
(Shake hands in front of your body.)
Shake, shake, shake.
(Shake hands in front of your body.)

Shake, shake, shake.
(Shake hands in front of your body.)
Shake it up high;
(Shake hands up high over your head.)
Shake it down low.
(Shake hands down low beside your knees.)
Shake, shake, shake.
(Shake hands in front of your body.)

 **Bible Story**

Sing for Joy

by Daphna Flegal

Have the children sit down in your story area. Tell the children the story and do the motions. Encourage the children to do the motions with you.

Whisper:
Shh, shh, shh! *(Put your finger in front of your lips.)* It was very early in the morning. Everything was quiet in the garden.

Shh, shh, shh! *(Put your finger in front of your lips.)* There was a tomb in this garden. A tomb is a place where they bury people.

Step, step, step. *(Pat your legs slowly.)* Two women came walking into the garden. Their steps were slow.

Step, step, step. *(Pat your legs slowly.)* The women were sad. Their friend, Jesus, was dead. He was buried in the tomb. A big rock was rolled in front of the door.

Speak in a louder voice:
Shake, shake, shake. *(Shake your hands in front of your body.)* Suddenly the ground began to shake! There was a great earthquake!

Shake, shake, shake. *(Shake your hands in front of your body.)* The two women felt the ground shaking. They were afraid.

Look, look, look. *(Point to far away.)* The women saw an angel. He seemed to glow with light.

Look, look, look. *(Point to far away.)* The angel rolled the big rock away from the door of the tomb.

Speak in a calm voice:
"Do not be afraid," *(Shake your head no.)* said the angel to the women. "You are looking for your friend, Jesus. But he is not here. He is alive."

"Do not be afraid," *(Shake your head no.)* said the angel to the women. "Go and tell all his friends that Jesus is alive!"

Speak in an excited voice:
Run, run, run. *(Pat your legs quickly.)* The two women ran quickly to tell all their friends that Jesus was alive!

Run, run, run. *(Pat your legs quickly.)* The two women were filled with great joy!

Bible Verse Fun

Choose a child to hold the Bible open to Psalm 98:4.

Say: Joy is one of the fruit of the Spirit. Our Bible story today is about the joy Jesus' friends felt when they knew Jesus was alive.

We celebrate with joy because we know Jesus is alive!

Say the Bible verse, "Sing for joy to the LORD, all the earth" (Psalm 98:4, GNT), for the children. Have the children say the Bible verse after you.

Help the children learn the Bible verse by singing. Sing the words printed below to the tune of "Hot Cross Buns."

"Sing for joy
To the Lord."
We are happy,
Oh, so happy.
"Sing for joy!"
© 1998 Abingdon Press

Let the children move to the Bible verse. Have the children stand in an open area of the room.

Say: Let's celebrate with joy. Every time you hear me say the word *joy*, jump up and down.

Say the Bible verse as suggested below. Have the children jump each time they hear the word joy.

Whisper: **Sing for joy.**
Shout: **Sing for joy.**
Whisper: **Sing for joy to the LORD.**
Shout: **Sing for joy to the LORD, all the earth.**

Supplies

Reproducible 2B, crayons, thinned blue tempera paint, plastic containers, paintbrushes, newspaper, smocks

All the Earth

Photocopy the Bible verse picture **(Reproducible 2B)** for each child. Cover the table with newspaper and have the children wear smocks to protect their clothing. Let the children decorate the pictures with crayons. Encourage the children to make heavy marks with the crayons.

Thin blue tempera paint with water. Pour the thinned paint into plastic containers. Let the children brush the paint all over their pictures. The crayon markings will show through the paint wash.

Read the Bible verse to the children.

Say: Joy is one of the fruit of the Spirit. Our Bible story today is about the joy Jesus' friends felt when they knew Jesus was alive.

> # We celebrate with joy because we know Jesus is alive!

Supplies

mural paper or tablecloth paper, watercolor markers, tape, optional: CD of Christian music, CD player

Joy Jiggles

Place mural paper or tablecloth paper on the table or floor. Use a watercolor marker to write the word JOY across the paper.

Say: Joy is one of the fruit of the Spirit. Our Bible story today is about the joy Jesus' friends felt when they knew Jesus was alive. Let's make a colorful banner for the word joy.

Let each child choose a marker. Sing the Bible verse song (page 25) for the children. Encourage the children to use the watercolor markers to make jiggly, squiggly lines as you sing.

Stop singing. Have each child choose a different color marker. Sing the song again and have the children make more squiggles with the new color. Continue as long as the children show interest. Display the banner in your classroom or in the hall.

If you are uncomfortable singing for the children, play a CD of Christian music.

Fruit Roll-ups

Have the children sit in a circle with their legs spread apart.

Say: A man named Paul wrote a letter to his friends about how we grow when we learn about Jesus. "We are like a tree that grows fruit," wrote Paul. "But our fruit is not the kind of fruit we eat. It is not apples and bananas and grapes. The fruit of the Spirit is love, joy, peace, patience, kindness, generosity, faithfulness, gentleness, and self-control." Today we are learning about joy.

(*Child's name*), God's Spirit gives you joy.

Roll the ball to the child you named. Have the child repeat the word *joy* and then roll the ball back to you. Continue around the circle until each child has a turn saying the word and rolling the ball.

Fruit of the Spirit Prayers

Have the children stand in a circle.

Say: Today we heard the Bible story about the joy Jesus' friends felt when they knew that Jesus was alive. Joy is a fruit of the Spirit. Listen to a poem about the fruit of the Spirit. Say the words of the poem after me and do what I do.

Love, joy, peace
are words that show we care.
So give a hug, (*Hug yourself.*)
laugh out loud, (*Put your hands on your stomach and shake.*)
then say a quiet prayer. (*Fold hands in prayer.*)

Patience, kindness, generosity
remind us what to do.
Wait for our turn, (*Stand still.*)
act with love, (*Point to your heart.*)
and share with others too. (*Move arms out as if presenting a gift.*)

Faithfulness, gentleness, self-control
are three big words to know.
Trust our great God, (*Cross your hands over your heart.*)
use kind words, (*Cup hands around mouth.*)
and choose right as we grow. (*Squat down and then stretch up tall.*)

© 2008 Abingdon Press

Pray: Thank you, God, for the joy we feel when we remember that Jesus is alive. Amen.

Jump for Joy!

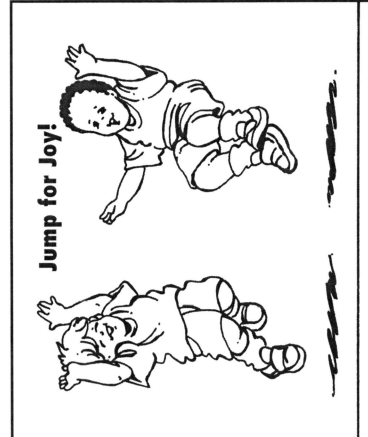

Super Stretch!

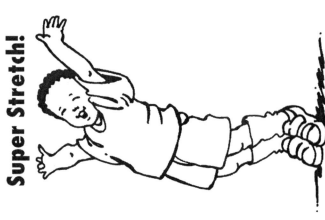

Happy Hop!

Gallop With Glee!

REPRODUCIBLE 2A

Sing for joy to the Lord!
all the earth.
Psalm 98:4 Good News Bible

REPRODUCIBLE 2B

Peace

Bible Verse

Happy are those who work for peace.
Matthew 5:9, GNT

Bible Story

Galatians 5:22–23; 1 Samuel 25:2–43

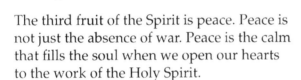

The third fruit of the Spirit is peace. Peace is not just the absence of war. Peace is the calm that fills the soul when we open our hearts to the work of the Holy Spirit.

The story of Abigail and David is a perfect example of peace. Hospitality was considered a duty in David's time. During the time of the sheep-shearing festival, David and his armies had been camped near the place where Nabal's flocks were grazing. By camping there, they had protected Nabal's valuable flocks from thieves. David asked Nabal if he and his men could be given food and drink in exchange for this help.

Nabal treated David's men with disrespect and denied their request. This was a major breach of Middle Eastern hospitality.

David, young and rather hot-tempered, was angered by Nabal's rejection. David decided to respond by destroying Nabal.

When one of Nabal's shepherds who had been protected by David found out what was going to happen, he went to Abigail, Nabal's wife.

Abigail realized that her husband's response put them all in danger. Even though David's response was a rash overreaction, Abigail saw that something must be done.

Abigail deliberately chose peace over winning the argument. She gave David and his men more provisions than were asked for in the original request. She then bowed humbly before David and asked David's forgiveness for her husband's foolishness.

Abigail kept peace not only for her family, but also for David and his men, by showing that disputes can be settled when people are generous and are willing to forgo the victory of proving they were right. Peace is not a passive act; it requires courage and faith.

God wants us to work for peace.

If time is limited, we recommend those activities that are noted in **boldface**. Depending on your time and the number of children, you may be able to include more activities.

ACTIVITY	TIME	SUPPLIES
Fruit Fun	**5 minutes**	**Reproducible 1A, scissors**
Colors of Peace	5 minutes	Reproducible 3A, crayons or markers
Shake 'n Celebrate	5 minutes	None
Bible Story: The Peacemaker	**10 minutes**	**None**
Bible Verse Fun	**5 minutes**	**Bible, chair**
Peace Painting	15 minutes	Reproducible 3B, large bowl, flour, salt, water, newspaper, smocks, white liquid tempera paint, plastic squeeze bottles; or white feathers, glue
Peaceful Lessons	10 minutes	play dough or clay
Fruit Roll-ups	5 minutes	ball
Fruit of the Spirit Prayers	**5 minutes**	**None**

JOIN THE FUN

BIBLE STORY FUN

LIVE THE FUN

JOIN THE FUN

Fruit Fun

Supplies

Reproducible
1A, scissors

Photocopy and cut apart at least two sets of the fruit pictures from Lesson 1 **(Reproducible 1A, page 18)**. Mix up the pictures and place them on a table or rug. Let the children enjoy matching the pictures.

Ask: What do you see in these pictures? *(fruit)*

Say: These fruits are called the fruit of the Spirit. A man named Paul wrote a letter to his friends about how we grow when we learn about Jesus. "We are like a tree that grows fruit," wrote Paul. "But our fruit is not the kind of fruit we eat. It is not apples and bananas and grapes. The fruit of the Spirit is love, joy, peace, patience, kindness, generosity, faithfulness, gentleness, and self-control." Peace is one of the fruit of the Spirit. God's Spirit gives us peace to help us live the way God wants us to live. Our Bible story today is about a woman named Abigail. Abigail was a peacemaker. She worked for peace.

> ## God wants us to work for peace.

Supplies

Reproducible
3A, crayons or
markers

Colors of Peace

Photocopy the coloring page of Abigail **(Reproducible 3A)**. Let the children decorate the pictures with crayons or markers.

Say: Our Bible story today is about a woman named Abigail. *(Point to the picture of Abigail.)* **Abigail was a peacemaker.** *(Point to the picture of the donkey.)* **I wonder why Abigail is leading a donkey? What is on the donkey's back?** *(food, bread)* **We will hear why Abigail has a donkey loaded with food in today's Bible story.**

Display the children's pictures in your story area.

Say: Peace is one of the fruit of the Spirit. Our Bible story today is about a woman named Abigail. Abigail was a peacemaker. She worked for peace.

> ## God wants us to work for peace.

32

Shake 'n Celebrate

Supplies

None

Say: Peace is one of the fruit of the Spirit. Our Bible story today is about a woman named Abigail. Abigail worked for peace.

> ## God wants us to work for peace.

Have the children move to an open area of the room. Say the following action poem and do the motions with the children.

Shake, shake, shake,
(Shake hands in front of your body.)
Shake, shake, shake.
(Shake hands in front of your body.)
Shake it up high;
(Shake hands up high over your head.)
Shake it down low.
(Shake hands down low beside your knees.)
Shake, shake, shake.
(Shake hands in front of your body.)

A fruit of the Spirit is peace.
(Place hands over your heart.)
Let's shake, shake, shake for peace.
(Shake hands in front of your body.)
Shake it up high;
(Shake hands up high over your head.)
Shake it down low.
(Shake hands down low beside your knees.)
Shake, shake, shake for peace.
(Shake hands in front of your body.)
Shake, shake, shake.
(Shake hands in front of your body.)

Shake, shake, shake.
(Shake hands in front of your body.)
Shake it up high;
(Shake hands up high over your head.)
Shake it down low.
(Shake hands down low beside your knees.)
Shake, shake, shake.
(Shake hands in front of your body.)

The Peacemaker

by Daphna Flegal

Tell the children the story. Have the children repeat the sentences printed in bold.

Nabal was a very rich man. He had many, many sheep and many, many goats. But Nabal was also very mean.

Nabal was mean, grrr, grrr! *(Have the children growl in a mean voice.)*

Nabal had a beautiful wife. Her name was Abigail. She was very kind and very smart.

Abigail was a peacemaker, oh yes! *(Have the children say, "Oh yes!")*

David was the man in charge of an army. David and his men were camping near Nabal's home.

David was a fighter, oh no! *(Have the children say, "Oh no!")*

One day Nabal was out cutting the wool from his sheep. David and his men were hungry. David sent ten of his young men to ask Nabal for bread and water and meat.

"Peace be to you," said the men. "We are David's men. We have been camping near your sheep. We have not harmed your sheep or the people taking care of your sheep. We did not take anything from you. We helped keep your sheep safe. Please share some bread and water and meat with us."

"I don't know anyone named David," said Nabal in a mean voice. "Why should I give you any food? Go away!"

Nabal was mean, grrr, grrr! *(Have the children growl in a mean voice.)*

David's men hurried back to the camp. They told David what Nabal had said. David became angry.

"Everyone, put on your swords," shouted David. "We are going to fight Nabal."

David was a fighter, oh no! *(Have the children say, "Oh no!")*

One of Nabal's servants ran to Abigail. He told her what Nabal had said to David's men.

Abigail quickly started packing food on donkeys. She packed bread and water and meat. Abigail rode one of the donkeys to David and his men. She got off the donkey and talked to David.

"Please don't fight," said Abigail. "I have brought you bread and water and meat for all your men."

David took the food. "Don't worry," said David. "We will not fight. You are safe."

Abigail was a peacemaker, oh yes! *(Have the children say, "Oh yes!")*

Bible Verse Fun

Choose a child to hold the Bible open to Matthew 5:9.

Say: Peace is one of the fruit of the Spirit. Our Bible story today is about a woman named Abigail. Abigail was a peacemaker.

Say the Bible verse, "Happy are those who work for peace" (Matthew 5:9, GNT), for the children. Have the children say the Bible verse after you.

God wants us to work for peace.

Help the children learn the Bible verse by singing. Sing the words printed below to the tune of "This Is the Way."

> "Happy are those who work for peace,"
> Work for peace, work for peace.
> "Happy are those who work for peace,"
> We can work for peace.

Let the children move to the Bible verse. Place a chair in the middle of the room.

Choose one child to sit in the chair. Have the remaining children make a circle around the chair.

Say: (*Name of child sitting in the chair*), you can work for peace.

Let the children walk in a circle and sing the Bible verse song again using the child's name in the last line,

> "Happy are those who work for peace,"
> Work for peace, work for peace.
> "Happy are those who work for peace,"
> (*Child's name*) can work for peace.

Continue the game until everyone has had a turn sitting in the chair.

Supplies

Reproducible 3B, large bowl, flour, salt, water, newspaper, smocks, white liquid tempera paint, plastic squeeze bottles; or white feathers, glue

Peace Painting

Let the children make puffy paint. Cover the table with newspaper and have the children wear smocks to protect their clothing. Mix equal parts flour, salt, and water in a large bowl. Add white liquid tempera to color the mixture. Pour the paint into plastic squeeze bottles.

Photocopy the dove picture (Reproducible 3B) for each child. Let the children squeeze the puffy paint onto their pictures to decorate their doves.

Or, if you choose not to make puffy paint, let the children glue white craft feathers onto their doves.

Say: Sometimes we use pictures of doves to remind us of peace. Peace is a fruit of the Spirit.

God wants us to work for peace.

Supplies

play dough or clay

Peaceful Lessons

Provide play dough or clay. Give each child a portion of the dough or clay. Do not encourage the children to share, as that can also share germs. Place each child's play dough or clay in a resealable plastic bag and send the play dough or clay home with the child.

Talk with the children while they are working with the play dough or clay about what makes them feel angry or frustrated. Help the children realize that there are things they can do to work for peace when they are feeling angry or frustrated. Go over the suggestions listed below with the children.

• Walk away from the situation and come back to it later.
• Get some help from someone.
• Try doing what you are doing in a different way.
• Relax. Sing a song, take a deep breath, get some water, take a walk.
• Use words rather than hitting or screaming or pushing. Let your words tell how angry you are.

Reprinted from *Wonder-filled Weekdays for Fall*, by Millie S. Goodson. © 1999 Abingdon Press.

Fruit Roll-ups

Have the children sit in a circle with their legs spread apart.

Say: A man named Paul wrote a letter to his friends about how we grow when we learn about Jesus. "We are like a tree that grows fruit," wrote Paul. "But our fruit is not the kind of fruit we eat. It is not apples and bananas and grapes. The fruit of the Spirit is love, joy, peace, patience, kindness, generosity, faithfulness, gentleness, and self-control." Today we are learning about peace.

(Child's name), God's Spirit gives you peace.

Roll the ball to the child you named. Have the child repeat the word *peace* and then roll the ball back to you. Continue around the circle until each child has a turn saying the word and rolling the ball.

Fruit of the Spirit Prayers

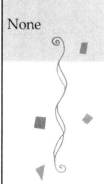

Have the children stand in a circle.

Say: Today we heard the Bible story about peace. Abigail was a pecemaker; she worked for peace. Peace is a fruit of the Spirit. Listen to a poem about the fruit of the Spirit. Say the words of the poem after me and do what I do.

Love, joy, peace
are words that show we care.
So give a hug, (Hug yourself.)
laugh out loud, (Put your hands on your stomach and shake.)
then say a quiet prayer. (Fold hands in prayer.)

Patience, kindness, generosity
remind us what to do.
Wait for our turn, (Stand still.)
act with love, (Point to your heart.)
and share with others too. (Move arms out as if presenting a gift.)

Faithfulness, gentleness, self-control
are three big words to know.
Trust our great God, (Cross your hands over your heart.)
use kind words, (Cup hands around mouth.)
and choose right as we grow. (Squat down and then stretch up tall.)

© 2008 Abingdon Press

Pray: Thank you, God, for helping us work for peace. Thank you for our friends (name each child and teacher). Amen.

ALL–IN–ONE BIBLE FUN

Fruit of the Spirit - Preschool

All-in-One

BIBLE PRESCHOOL

FUN

Patience

Bible Verse

Be patient and wait for the LORD to act.

Psalm 37:7, GNT

Bible Story

Galatians 5:22–23; Genesis 17:1–16; 18:1–15; 21:1–7

Patience is the fourth fruit of the Spirit listed in Galatians 5:22–23. Patience requires endurance, quiet perseverance, and hope. Patience believes in God's guiding presence and abiding love. If anyone ever needed patience, it was Abraham and Sarah.

Twenty-five years had passed since God first promised to make of Abram a great nation. Now God was speaking again. Abram's and Sarai's names were changed to Abraham and Sarah as a symbol of God's covenant with them. God's covenant was an everlasting covenant to be the God of a great people descended from Abraham and Sarah.

Abraham—at the ripe old age of ninety-nine—had a good laugh at this. This didn't seem like a likely possibility but God promised that in one year Sarah would bear a son.

Sarah was having doubts that God was going to come through with that all-important child. After all, how can one have

descendants without having children? Time, by all human standards, had already run out for her childbearing years.

Abraham and Sarah lived in the desert. Visitors were welcomed because to deny a visitor food and water might result in the visitor's death. Abraham greeted three visitors and wound up entertaining God. The promise that Sarah would bear a son was given again. This time it was Sarah who laughed.

Abraham's and Sarah's patience and obedience were rewarded. God's promise was finally fulfilled, and a son was born to Abraham and Sarah. He was named Isaac, whose name means "laughter." Sarah rejoiced, "God has brought laughter for me; everyone who hears will laugh with me" (Genesis 21:6).

Patience is not easy for preschool children, who are just learning about waiting and taking turns. Help them understand that there are times when everyone must have patience.

We can be patient and trust God.

If time is limited, we recommend those activities that are noted in **boldface**. Depending on your time and the number of children, you may be able to include more activities.

ACTIVITY	TIME	SUPPLIES	
Fruit Tray	5 minutes	tray, towel or cloth, plastic fruit or Reproducible 1A, scissors	JOIN THE FUN
Patience Power	**5 minutes**	**Reproducible 4A, scissors**	
Guess What?	5 minutes	Reproducible 4B, tape	BIBLE STORY FUN
Be Patient, Be Patient	5 minutes	None	
Bible Story: Ha, Ha, Ha	**10 minutes**	**Reproducible 4B**	
Bible Verse Fun	**5 minutes**	**Bible**	
The Laughing Game	5 minutes	None	
Wait Your Turn	10 minutes	newspaper, trash can, masking tape	
Fruit Roll-ups	5 minutes	ball	LIVE THE FUN
Fruit of the Spirit Prayers	**5 minutes**	**None**	

Supplies

tray, towel or cloth, plastic fruit or Reproducible 1A, scissors

Fruit Tray

Place the plastic fruit on a tray. (If you do not have plastic fruit, photocopy and cut apart the fruit pictures from **Reproducible 1A**. Place the fruit pictures on the tray). Name the different fruits for the children. Cover the fruit with a towel or cloth. Have the children cover their eyes. Remove one of the fruits from underneath the cloth and hide it from the children. Have the children open their eyes. Uncover the tray and have the children try to remember which fruit is missing.

Continue the game as long as the children show interest. If the game is easy for the children, make it more challenging by taking away two or three fruits at a time.

Say: These fruits are called the fruit of the Spirit. A man named Paul wrote a letter to his friends about how we grow when we learn about Jesus. "We are like a tree that grows fruit," wrote Paul. "But our fruit is not the kind of fruit we eat. It is not apples and bananas and grapes. The fruit of the Spirit is love, joy, peace, patience, kindness, generosity, faithfulness, gentleness, and self-control." Patience is one of the fruit of the Spirit. God's Spirit gives us patience to help us live the way God wants us to live. Our Bible story today is about a man named Abraham and a woman named Sarah. Abraham and Sarah had to wait a long time for something God promised them. They were patient and trusted God.

> **We can be patient and trust God.**

Supplies

Reproducible 4A, scissors

Patience Power

Photocopy and cut apart at least two sets of the cards that show things we have to wait for **(Reproducible 4A)**. Mix up the pictures and place them on a table or rug. Let the children enjoy matching the pictures.

Ask: **What is happening in these pictures?** *(They show things we have to wait for: waiting in line at the water fountain; waiting to get a hamburger; waiting for a birthday; waiting for Christmas; waiting for a baby to be born; waiting for Dad to come home.)*

Say: Patience is one of the fruit of the Spirit. Patience means being willing to wait. We wait our turn; we wait for our birthdays; and we wait for Christmas.

Guess What?

Reproducible 4B, tape

Photocopy the baby Isaac picture **(Reproducible 4B)**. Fold the paper along the dotted line so that baby Isaac is inside and tape the paper shut. Show the children the folded paper.

Say: Our Bible story today is about a man named Abraham and a woman named Sarah. Abraham and Sarah had to wait a long time for something God promised them. Inside this card is a picture of what Abraham and Sarah were waiting for. Can you guess what is on the picture inside the paper?

Encourage each child to guess what is pictured inside the folded paper.

Say: We have to wait until it's time for the Bible story to find out what's inside.

Be Patient, Be Patient

None

Have the children move to an open area of the room. Lead the children in the following action poem.

I want to eat my supper,
(Pretend to eat.)
Oh me, oh my, oh wow.
(Touch your toes; touch your shoulders; hold arms above head.)
I want to eat my supper,
(Pretend to eat.)
And I want to eat right now!
(Put hands on hips.)

I want to go to my friend's house,
(Walk in place.)
Oh me, oh my, oh wow.
(Touch your toes; touch your shoulders; hold arms above head.)
I want to go to my friend's house,
(Walk in place.)
And I want to go right now!
(Put hands on hips.)

Be patient, be patient,
(Fold hands in front of your body.)
Even though it seems so late.
(Cross arms; tap foot.)
Be patient, be patient,
(Fold hands in front of your body.)
Breathe deeply while you wait.
(Take a deep breath to relax.)

Be patient, be patient,
(Fold hands in front of your body.)
Even though it seems so late.
(Cross arms; tap foot.)
Be patient, be patient,
(Fold hands in front of your body.)
Breathe deeply while you wait.
(Take a deep breath to relax.)

We can be patient and trust God.

Ha, Ha, Ha

by LeeDell Stickler and Daphna Flegal

Have the children sit down in your story area. Copy the baby Isaac picture (Reproducible 4B) and fold along the dotted line so the image is inside. Show the children the folded picture of baby Isaac. Have the children tell you what they guess the picture inside the folded paper is. Open the paper and show them the picture of baby Isaac.

Say: Our Bible story today is about a man named Abraham and a woman named Sarah. Abraham and Sarah had to wait a long time for something God promised them. They waited and waited to have a son.

Tell the children the story. Have the children repeat, "Ha, ha, ha. Ha, ha, ha," and do the motions.

Once, a long, long time ago, there lived a man named Abraham and his wife, Sarah. They lived in a country far, far away. They had a happy life, except that they didn't have any children.

One day God spoke to Abraham. "I want you to leave this home and go to a land that I will show you. If you do this, I will give you many children and grandchildren."

Ha, ha, ha. Ha, ha, ha. *(Hold stomach; shake.)*

Abraham and Sarah laughed. They were very old—much too old to be having children. But Abraham and Sarah trusted God. So they packed up all their belongings and set off to the new land that God would show them. And they waited for God to keep the promise.

Time passed. Abraham and Sarah grew even older. One day Abraham and Sarah came to a beautiful land. God told them, "One day all this land will belong to your children and to their children."

Ha, ha, ha. Ha, ha, ha. *(Hold stomach; shake.)*

Abraham and Sarah laughed. They knew that they were very old. They also knew that they didn't have any children—yet. But they trusted God, and they waited for God to keep the promise.

More time passed. Abraham and Sarah grew even older. One day God sent messengers to tell Abraham that soon he and Sarah would have a baby boy.

Ha, ha, ha. Ha, ha, ha. *(Hold stomach; shake.)*

Sarah overheard what the messengers said. She began to laugh and laugh and laugh. She knew that God had promised her a child. But she was over ninety years old. She was too old to have a baby.

But God kept the promise. Abraham and Sarah had a beautiful son.

Ha, ha, ha. Ha, ha, ha. *(Hold stomach; shake.)*

Sarah named her son Isaac, whose name means "laughter."

Every time Abraham and Sarah looked at their baby, they remembered God's promise. They remembered to be patient and to trust God.

Bible Verse Fun

Choose a child to hold the Bible open to Psalm 37:7.

Say: Patience is one of the fruit of the Spirit. Our Bible story today is about a man named Abraham and a woman named Sarah. Abraham and Sarah had to wait a long time for the baby son God promised them. They were patient and trusted God.

Say the Bible verse, "Be patient and wait for the LORD to act" (Psalm 37:7, GNT), for the children. Have the children say the Bible verse after you.

> ## We can be patient and trust God.

Help the children learn the Bible verse by singing. Sing the words printed below to the tune of "The Wheels on the Bus."

> "Be patient and wait for the LORD to act,
> LORD to act, LORD to act."
> "Be patient and wait for the LORD to act."
> Trust in the LORD.

Let the children move to the Bible verse. Have the children sit down on the floor.

Say: I am going to name some things we have to wait for. Listen carefully. When I say, "Be patient," I want you to stand up and say, "Wait for the LORD to act." Then sit back down.

Teacher: **We wait for our birthdays to come each year.**
We wait for supper time to be here.
Be patient ...
Children: **Wait for the LORD to act.**

Teacher: **We wait for new babies to be born.**
We wait to celebrate Christmas morn.
Be patient ...
Children: **Wait for the LORD to act.**

Teacher: **We wait for the rain coming down to stop.**
We wait for the popcorn to heat up and pop.
Be patient ...
Children: **Wait for the LORD to act.**

Supplies

None

The Laughing Game

Have the children join you on the rug or in an open area of the room. Choose one child to lie down on the floor, face up. Have the next child lie down with his or her head resting on the first child's stomach. The third person rests his head on the stomach of the second person, and so on.

As each child lies down, the person or persons on the floor begins saying, "Ha, ha."

As each child joins the group, words of laughter will become true laughter as heads bounce on laughing stomachs. Join the game yourself after all of the other children are involved.

Say: God promised Sarah and Abraham that they would have children. They waited and waited and grew very old. Then God sent messengers to tell Abraham that Sarah would soon have a son. Sarah laughed when she heard the message because she was ninety years old, too old to have a baby. But God kept the promise, and Sarah had baby Isaac.

Supplies

newspaper,
trash can,
masking tape

Wait Your Turn

Give each child a piece of newspaper. Show the children how to crumple the newspaper to make a ball.

Place a trash can in an open area of the room. Place a piece of masking tape on the floor a short distance away from the trash can. Have the children line up behind the line of tape. Show the children how to toss the paper balls into the trash can. Let the children stand in line and take turns tossing the the balls. Do not keep score.

Go to each child in line while he or she is waiting for a turn.

Say things like: I like the way you are waiting for your turn. You are being very patient. Patience is a fruit of the Spirit. Sometimes it's hard to wait for things, but your turn will come soon.

Remind the children that Abraham and Sarah had to wait a long time for the baby son God promised them. They were patient and trusted God.

Fruit Roll-ups

Supplies

ball

Have the children sit in a circle with their legs spread apart.

Say: **A man named Paul wrote a letter to his friends about how we grow when we learn about Jesus. "We are like a tree that grows fruit," wrote Paul. "But our fruit is not the kind of fruit we eat. It is not apples and bananas and grapes. The fruit of the Spirit is love, joy, peace, patience, kindness, generosity, faithfulness, gentleness, and self-control." Today we are learning about patience.**

(*Child's name***), God's Spirit gives you patience.**

Roll the ball to the child you named. Have the child repeat the word *patience* and then roll the ball back to you. Continue around the circle until each child has a turn saying the word and rolling the ball.

Fruit of the Spirit Prayers

Supplies

None

Have the children stand in a circle.

Say: **Abraham and Sarah had to wait a long time for the baby son God promised them. They were patient and trusted God. Patience is a fruit of the Spirit. Listen to a poem about the fruit of the Spirit. Say the words of the poem after me and do what I do.**

Love, joy, peace
are words that show we care.
So give a hug, *(Hug yourself.)*
laugh out loud, *(Put your hands on your stomach and shake.)*
then say a quiet prayer. *(Fold hands in prayer.)*

Patience, kindness, generosity
remind us what to do.
Wait for our turn, *(Stand still.)*
act with love, *(Point to your heart.)*
and share with others too. *(Move arms out as if presenting a gift.)*

Faithfulness, gentleness, self-control
are three big words to know.
Trust our great God, *(Cross your hands over your heart.)*
use kind words, *(Cup hands around mouth.)*
and choose right as we grow. *(Squat down and then stretch up tall.)*

Pray: **Thank you, God, for helping us be patient. Thank you for our friends (***name each child and teacher***). Amen.**

REPRODUCIBLE 4A

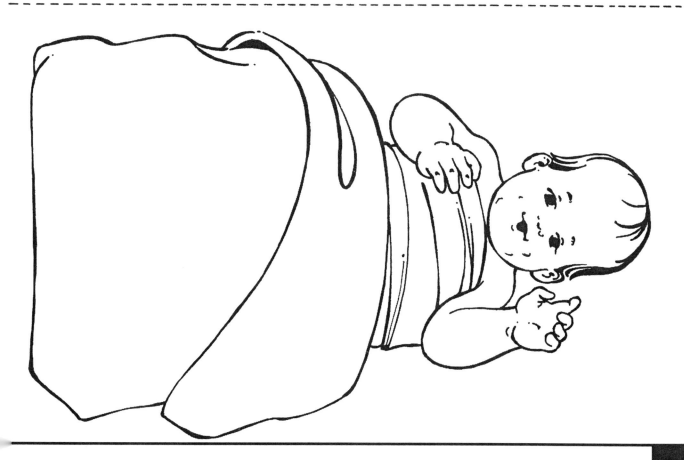

REPRODUCIBLE 4B

49

All-in-One

BIBLE PRESCHOOL

FUN

Kindness

Bible Verse

Be kind to one another.

Ephesians 4:32

Bible Story

Galatians 5:22–23; Luke 6:6–11; Matthew 12:9–14;
Mark 3:1–6

Galatians 5:22–23 lists kindness as the fifth fruit of the Spirit. Kindness is going beyond any expectations, cheerfully and lovingly. Kindness is not usually planned, but rather is a spur-of-the-moment prompting of the Holy Spirit.

In the Gospels the story is told of Jesus curing the withered hand of a man on the sabbath. Jesus healed many people during his ministry. His kindness toward all of God's people is shown in the many stories of his love and compassion. Jesus healed lepers, ate in the home of Mary and Martha, raised Lazarus from the dead, and changed the life of Zacchaeus. However, the story of the man with the paralyzed hand is an act that angered religious leaders of the day, specifically because Jesus was healing on the sabbath, a day of rest.

Why was this such a problem? Today healing is done routinely on every day of the week. Did Jesus merely set aside the laws of the

sabbath for more humanitarian purposes? This story goes straight to the authority of Jesus and his actions in the name of God. Jesus healed the withered hand because God has concern and compassion for God's children at all times. God has shown through Jesus that God's love and compassion is more important than rituals, even those commanded by God.

The old way of doing things was altered to show kindness to one of God's people who greatly needed it. Jesus showed us that God's compassion comes first.

As Christians, can we do less than to follow Jesus' example and to show kindness to any of God's people, no matter when that might be?

Encourage your children to be kind to others. Compliment the children when you see them do spontaneous acts of kindness.

We can be kind to one another.

If time is limited, we recommend those activities that are noted in **boldface**. Depending on your time and the number of children, you may be able to include more activities.

ACTIVITY	TIME	SUPPLIES
Fruit Tray	5 minutes	tray, towel or cloth, plastic fruit or Reproducible 1A, scissors
Kind Hands	**10 minutes**	**Reproducible 5A, newspaper, smocks, tempera paint, paintbrushes, shallow trays, hand-washing supplies**
The Kindness Train	5 minutes	None
Bible Story: Be Kind	**10 minutes**	**None**
Bible Verse Fun	**10 minutes**	**Bible, 12 pieces of paper, marker, optional: CD of Christian music, CD player**
Kindness Capers	10 minutes	None
Bible Verse Bracelets	10 minutes	Reproducible 5B, scissors, crayons or markers, tape
Fruit of the Spirit Prayers	**5 minutes**	**None**

JOIN THE FUN

BIBLE STORY FUN

LIVE THE FUN

JOIN THE FUN

Supplies

tray, towel or cloth, plastic fruit or Reproducible 1A, scissors

Fruit Tray

Place the plastic fruit on a tray. (If you do not have plastic fruit, photocopy and cut apart the fruit pictures from **Reproducible 1A**. Place the fruit pictures on the tray). Name the different fruits for the children. Cover the fruit with a towel or cloth. Have the children cover their eyes. Remove one of the fruits from underneath the cloth and hide it from the children. Have the children open their eyes. Uncover the tray and have the children try to remember which fruit is missing.

Continue the game as long as the children show interest. If the game is easy for the children, make it more challenging by taking away two or three fruits at a time.

Say: **These fruits can help us remember the fruit of the Spirit. Jesus taught us how to live the way God wants us to live. God wants us to be kind. Kindness is one of the fruit of the Spirit. Our Bible story today is about Jesus and a man who could not move his hand. Jesus healed the man's hand so that it could move again. Jesus was kind to the man.**

> ## We can be kind to one another.

Supplies

Reproducible 5A, newspaper, smocks, tempera paint, paintbrushes, shallow trays, handwashing supplies

Kind Hands

Photocopy the Bible verse page **(Reproducible 5A)** for each child. Let the children decorate the Bible verse by adding their handprints.

Cover the table with newspaper and have the children wear smocks. Pour tempera paint into shallow trays. Have each child stretch out a hand. Use a paintbrush to paint the child's palm. You may want to paint each finger a different color. Then have the child press her or his hand onto the Bible verse page. Have the children wash their hands. Set their handprints aside to dry.

Say: **Kindness is one of the fruit of the Spirit. Our Bible story today is about Jesus and a man who could not move his hand. Jesus healed the man's hand so that it could move again. Jesus was kind to the man. We can be kind to one another.**

The Kindness Train

Say: Kindness is one of the fruit of the Spirit.

Supplies

None

We can be kind to one another.

Lead the children in the following movement activity. Encourage the children to make a train and to move around the room. End the movement in your story area.

Come follow me and make a train.
(Have each child stand behind you to make a train.)
Come follow me right now.
Stretch out your hands
*(Have each child touch the shoulders
of the person in front of him or her.)*
To make a train.
I'm sure you all know how.

Get on board the kindness train.
(Keep adding children until everyone is participating.)
Get on board right now.
Stretch out your hands
*(Have each child touch the shoulders
of the person in front of him or her.)*
To make a train.
I'm sure you all know how.

Choo, choo, choo.
Chug, chug, chug.
Around the room we go.
(Shuffle around the room.)

Choo, choo, choo.
Chug, chug, chug.
For kindness we can show.
(Shuffle around the room.)

Be kind. Be kind.
(Keep repeating.)

Be Kind

by Daphna Flegal

Say: Kindness is one of the fruit of the Spirit. Our Bible story today is about Jesus and a man who could not move his hand. Jesus healed the man's hand so that the man could move it. Jesus was kind to the man.

Tell the children the story and have the children do the motions with you each time you say the refrain.

Be kind,
(Stretch out one arm.)
Be kind,
(Stretch out other arm.)
Be kind to one another.
(Cross both arms over chest.)

Jesus went to the synagogue,
To read God's Word and pray.
Others went to watch him,
And hear what he had to say.

Be kind,
(Stretch out one arm.)
Be kind,
(Stretch out other arm.)
Be kind to one another.
(Cross both arms over chest.)

A man was at the synagogue
Who could not move one hand.
He could not move his fingers
Or make a handprint in the sand.

Be kind,
(Stretch out one arm.)
Be kind,
(Stretch out other arm.)
Be kind to one another.
(Cross both arms over chest.)

Jesus stood in the synagogue
And saw that the man was there.
Jesus knew just what to do
To show God's love and care.

Be kind,
(Stretch out one arm.)
Be kind,
(Stretch out other arm.)
Be kind to one another.
(Cross both arms over chest.)

"Stretch out your hand," Jesus said.
"Now do what I command."
And slowly, slowly, inch by inch,
The man stretched out his hand.

Be kind,
(Stretch out one arm.)
Be kind,
(Stretch out other arm.)
Be kind to one another.
(Cross both arms over chest.)

So right there in the synagogue
Jesus healed the man that day,
While others stood and watched him
Show that kindness was God's way.

Be kind,
(Stretch out one arm.)
Be kind,
(Stretch out other arm.)
Be kind to one another.
(Cross both arms over chest.)

Bible Verse Fun

Choose a child to hold the Bible open to Ephesians 4:32.

Say: Kindness is one of the fruit of the Spirit. Our Bible story today is about Jesus and a man who could not move his hand. Jesus healed the man's hand so that it could move again. Jesus was kind to the man.

We can be kind to one another.

Say the Bible verse, "Be kind to one another" (Ephesians 4:32), for the children. Have the children say the Bible verse after you.

Help the children learn the Bible verse by singing. Sing the words printed below to the tune of "London Bridge."

> The Bible tells us to be kind,
> To be kind, to be kind.
> The Bible tells us to be kind,
> "Be kind to one another."
> © 1998 Abingdon Press

Let the children move to the Bible verse. Write the numbers 1 through 12, one number each on separate sheets of paper. The numbers should be as big as the page will allow.

Place the numbers in a big circle on the floor. Make it big enough so the children can walk "around the clock" without stepping on each other's heels.

Say: Our numbers look like a clock. A clock tells us what time it is.

Sing the Bible verse song printed above and have the children walk around the circle clockwise. Stop singing. Choose a child that is standing by a number to say what time it is. The child holds up the number and everyone (who knows numbers) can say what it is.

Ask: Is *(name the hour)* a good time to be kind? *(yes)*

Then have the child with the number think of something kind. The group may help. After the child names something kind, have everyone say the Bible verse together.

The child puts the number back down in the circle and the game continues.

If you are not comfortable singing for the children use a CD of Christian music and a CD player.

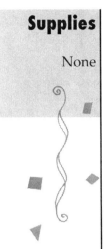

Supplies

None

Kindness Capers

Say: **Kindness is one of the fruit of the Spirit. Our Bible story today is about Jesus and a man who could not move his hand. Jesus healed the man's hand so that it could move again. Jesus was kind to the man.**

> ## We can be kind to one another.

Talk with the children about ways we can be kind, such as taking turns, sharing toys, helping clean up, saying "please" and "thank you," and so forth.

Say: **Listen to the things I say. If I say something that shows someone being kind, stretch your arms out and say, "Yes!" If I say something that shows someone not being kind, cross your arms over your chest and say, "No way!"**

Susie saw her mother bringing in bags of groceries from the car. Susie hurried to the door and opened the door for her mother. Was Susie kind?

(Stretch out your arms and say, "Yes!")

Maggie wanted to play with the trucks. She ran over and grabbed a truck away from Pat. Was Maggie kind?

(Cross your arms over your chest and say, "No way!")

Jacob sat down at the table for snack time. When his teacher gave him a cookie, he smiled and said, "Thank you." Was Jacob kind?

(Stretch out your arms and say, "Yes!")

Brad was playing with the blocks. He was building a big tower. Matt came over and kicked Brad's tower down. Was Matt kind?

(Cross your arms over your chest and say, "No way!")

Carrie and Caleb brought cans of food to church to share with people who did not have money to buy food. Were Carrie and Caleb kind?

(Stretch out your arms and say, "Yes!")

Bible Verse Bracelets

Supplies

Reproducible 5B, scissors, crayons or markers, tape

Photocopy and cut apart the Bible verse strips **(Reproducible 5B)**. Give each child a strip. Let the children decorate the strips with crayons or markers.

Say: **Stretch out your hand.**

Have each child stretch out a hand. Tape each child's bracelet around the child's wrist.

Say: **(Child's name), be kind to one another.**

Fruit of the Spirit Prayers

Supplies

None

Have the children stand in a circle.

Say: **Jesus was kind to the man who could not move his hand. Jesus healed the hand so it could move again. Kindness is a fruit of the Spirit. Listen to a poem about the fruit of the Spirit. Say the words of the poem after me and do what I do.**

Love, joy, peace
are words that show we care.
So give a hug, *(Hug yourself.)*
laugh out loud, *(Put your hands on your stomach and shake.)*
then say a quiet prayer. *(Fold hands in prayer.)*

Patience, kindness, generosity
remind us what to do.
Wait for our turn, *(Stand still.)*
act with love, *(Point to your heart.)*
and share with others too. *(Move arms out as if presenting a gift.)*

Faithfulness, gentleness, self-control
are three big words to know.
Trust our great God, *(Cross your hands over your heart.)*
use kind words, *(Cup hands around mouth.)*
and choose right as we grow. *(Squat down and then stretch up tall.)*

© 2008 Abingdon Press

Pray: **Thank you, God, for helping us be kind. Thank you for our friends** *(name each child and teacher)*. **Amen.**

Be kind to one another.

Ephesians 4:32

ALL-IN-ONE BIBLE FUN

REPRODUCIBLE 5B

All-in-One
BIBLE PRESCHOOL
FUN

Genererosity

Bible Verse

God loves a cheerful giver.

2 Corinthians 9:7

Bible Story

Galatians 5:22–23; Luke 21:1–4; Mark 12:41–44

Generosity is the sixth fruit of the Spirit listed in Galatians 5:22–23. Generosity is not only the willingness to give; it is also the willingness to give completely. The Holy Spirit guides us past our own needs and concerns to an awareness of and a response to the needs of others around us.

What makes a person generous? What is the true measure of a gift? These are questions that can be addressed by looking at the story of the widow's coins.

Outside of the Temple were thirteen receptacles to receive the gifts of the worshipers. There would be a loud clanging noise when the coins dropped. Jesus had been sitting, watching people drop coins into these receptacles. He would have had to hear all the noise these contributions made.

When the poor widow arrived and put her two copper coins in one of the receptacles, it would have been easy to hear that it was a very small amount.

The two copper coins were the smallest denominations of coins there were. Their value was very small. The rich who had been dropping large quantities of coins in the receptacles were giving out of their abundance. They could still afford large meals, lavish homes, and richly designed clothing. The widow would have none of these things, even if she kept her money. But the widow gave to God even that which she needed, while the rich gave out of their extra.

Jesus did not condemn the gift of the wealthy. What Jesus did was commend the extreme generosity of heart that caused the widow to give all she had to God. No gift of love is too small to count. Even the smallest gift can be the most generous gift. It depends upon the heart.

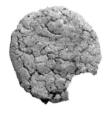

We can cheerfully give to others.

If time is limited, we recommend those activities that are noted in **boldface**. Depending on your time and the number of children, you may be able to include more activities.

ACTIVITY	TIME	SUPPLIES	
Fruit Tray	5 minutes	tray, towel or cloth, plastic fruit or Reproducible 1A, scissors	JOIN THE FUN
It's Fun to Share	**10 minutes**	**many different colors of construction paper, plain paper, glue**	
The Cheerful Train	5 minutes	None	BIBLE STORY FUN
Bible Story: Two Coins	**10 minutes**	**paper cups, plastic or real coins (14 for each child plus 21 for the leader)**	
Bible Verse Fun	**10 minutes**	**Bible, Reproducible 6A, scissors, masking tape**	
Cool Coins	15 minutes	Reproducible 6B, plastic or real coins, newspaper, smocks, tempera paint, shallow trays, paintbrushes, tape	
A Noisy Offering	10 minutes	clean coffee can or other metal container; paper; tape or glue; coins; crayons, markers, or happy face stickers	
Face It	10 minutes	chair	LIVE THE FUN
Fruit of the Spirit Prayers	**5 minutes**	**None**	

JOIN THE FUN

Supplies

tray, towel or cloth, plastic fruit or Reproducible 1A, scissors

Fruit Tray

Place the plastic fruit on a tray. (If you do not have plastic fruit, photocopy and cut apart the fruit pictures from **Reproducible 1A**. Place the fruit pictures on the tray). Name the different fruits for the children. Cover the fruit with a towel or cloth. Have the children cover their eyes. Remove one of the fruits from underneath the cloth and hide it from the children. Have the children open their eyes. Uncover the tray and have the children try to remember which fruit is missing.

Continue the game as long as the children show interest. If the game is easy for the children, make it more challenging by taking away two or three fruits at a time.

Say: These fruits can help us remember the fruit of the Spirit. God wants us to be generous. Generosity is one of the fruit of the Spirit. When we are generous, we are willing to give to others. We are willing to share. Our Bible story today is about a woman who was generous. She only had two coins, but she gave the two coins in an offering to God. She knew that "God loves a cheerful giver" (2 Corinthians 9:7).

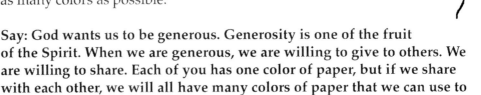

We can cheerfully give to others.

Supplies

many different colors of construction paper, plain paper, glue

It's Fun to Share

Give each child a different color of construction paper. Hand out as many colors as possible.

Say: God wants us to be generous. Generosity is one of the fruit of the Spirit. When we are generous, we are willing to give to others. We are willing to share. Each of you has one color of paper, but if we share with each other, we will all have many colors of paper that we can use to make pictures.

Encourage the children to tear their paper into several pieces and pile all the pieces together. If children are reluctant to share their paper, don't force them.

Give each child another piece of paper and invite them to choose scraps from the pile to glue onto their paper to make a colorful montage.

ALL–IN–ONE BIBLE FUN

The Cheerful Train

Supplies

None

Say: Generosity is one of the fruit of the Spirit. We are generous when we are cheerful givers. We are willing to share with others.

We can cheerfully give to others.

Lead the children in the following movement activity. Encourage the children to make a train and to move around the room. End the movement in your story area.

Come follow me and make a train.
(Have each child stand behind you to make a train.)
Come follow me right now.
Stretch out your hands
(Have each child touch the shoulders
of the person in front of him or her.)
To make a train.
I'm sure you all know how.

Get on board the cheerful train.
(Keep adding children until everyone is participating.)
Get on board right now.
Stretch out your hands
(Have each child touch the shoulders
of the person in front of him or her.)
To make a train.
I'm sure you all know how.

Choo, choo, choo.
Chug, chug, chug.
Around the room we go.
(Shuffle around the room.)

Choo, choo, choo.
Chug, chug, chug.
For generosity we can show.
(Shuffle around the room.)

Be a cheerful giver. Be a cheerful giver.
(Keep repeating.)

Two Coins

by Daphna Flegal

Have the children sit down at a table. Place fourteen coins and a paper cup in front of each child. You will need twenty-one coins and a paper cup. Have the children count with you and drop their coins into their paper cups as indicated in the story.

Be sure that the children keep the coins away from their noses, ears, and mouths.

1, 2, 3.
(Have each child drop three coins into the cup.)

Jesus watched a rich man drop three coins into the offering box. He heard the sound the three coins made. Jesus knew he had more coins at home.

Clang, clang, clang. It was a loud sound.

1, 2, 3, 4.
(Have each child drop four coins into the cup.)

Jesus watched a rich woman drop four coins into the offering box. He heard the sound the four coins made. Jesus knew she had more coins at home.

Clang, clang, clang, clang. It was a loud sound.

1, 2, 3, 4, 5.
(Have each child drop five coins into the cup.)

Jesus watched a rich man drop five coins into the offering box. He heard the sound the five coins made. Jesus knew he had more coins at home.

Clang, clang, clang, clang, clang. It was a very loud sound.

1, 2.
(Have each child drop two coins into the cup.)

Jesus watched a poor woman drop two coins in the offering box. He heard the sound the two coins made. Jesus knew she had no more coins at home.

Clang, clang. It was not a loud sound.

"This woman gave more than the others," said Jesus.

How can that be? *(Put two coins on the table or floor. Put three coins beside the two coins.)*

(Count the two coins.) **1, 2.** *(Count the three coins.)* **1, 2, 3.** Two coins are less than three coins.

(Add one more coin to the three coins. Count the two coins.) **1, 2.** *(Count the four coins.)* **1, 2, 3, 4.** Two coins are less than four coins.

(Add one more coin to the four coins. Count the two coins.) **1, 2.** *(Count the five coins.)* **1, 2, 3, 4, 5.** Two coins are less than five coins.

"This woman gave more," said Jesus, "because she gave all the coins she had."

Bible Verse Fun

Choose a child to hold the Bible open to 2 Corinthians 9:7.

Say: Generosity is one of the fruit of the Spirit. When we are generous, we are willing to give to others. We are willing to share. Our Bible story today is about a woman who was generous. She only had two coins, but she gave the two coins as an offering to God. She knew that "God loves a cheerful giver" (2 Corinthians 9:7).

We can cheerfully give to others.

Say the Bible verse, "God loves a cheerful giver" (2 Corinthians 9:7), for the children. Have the children say the Bible verse after you.

Help the children learn the Bible verse by singing. Sing the words printed below to the tune of "The Farmer in the Dell."

> "God loves a cheerful giver.
> God loves a cheerful giver."
> The Bible tells us how to give.
> "God loves a cheerful giver."

Let the children move to the Bible verse.

Photocopy the smiley face and smile **(Reproducible 6A)**. Cut out around the smile. Display the smiley face on a wall, bulletin board, or door. Be sure to place the picture where the children can easily reach it.

Say: Our Bible story today is about a woman who was generous. She only had two coins, but she gave the two coins in an offering to God. She knew that "God loves a cheerful giver" (2 Corinthians 9:7). Let's put a smile on this face to make it a cheerful giver.

Play the game like "Pin the Tail on the Donkey." Have the children come one at a time to stand in front of the face. Put a loop of masking tape on the back of the smile. Have each child close his or her eyes. Let the child try to place the smile where the mouth should be on the face.

After each child has placed the smile on the face, repeat the Bible verse with the child.

Supplies

Reproducible 6B, plastic or real coins, newspaper, smocks, tempera paint, shallow trays, paintbrushes, tape

Cool Coins

Photocopy the Bible verse page **(Reproducible 6B)** for each child. Cover the table with newspaper and have the children wear paint smocks to protect their clothing. Pour tempera paint into shallow trays.

Use a loop of tape to tape two coins in front of each child. Let the children use paintbrushes to brush tempera paint on their coins. Give each child a Bible verse page. Show the children how to place their papers face down on the coins and press over the paper. Gently remove the paper to see the print made from the coins.

Say: Generosity is one of the fruit of the Spirit. When we are generous, we are willing to give to others. We are willing to share. Our Bible story today is about a woman who was generous. She was willing to give all that she had. She only had two coins, but she gave the two coins in an offering to God.

We can cheerfully give to others.

Supplies

clean coffee can or other metal container; paper; tape or glue; coins; crayons, markers, or happy face stickers

A Noisy Offering

Provide a clean coffee can or other metal container. Wrap the outside of the container with paper. Secure the paper to the can with tape or glue. Show the children the offering container.

Say: In our Bible story today Jesus heard the sounds the coins made as people dropped the coins into the offering box. Let's make a noisy offering can for our room.

Let the children decorate the can by coloring with crayons or markers, by putting on happy face stickers, or by gluing some of the coins onto the paper. Drop a few coins into the can for the children to hear the sound.

Say: We will put any money you bring for an offering into our noisy offering can. We can remember that God loves a cheerful giver when we hear the noisy offering.

Face It

Supplies

chair

Say: Today's Bible verse is "God loves a cheerful giver" (2 Corinthians 9:7). **Say it with me.** *(Have the children repeat the Bible verse.)* **Not a grouchy giver, not a sleepy giver, not a silly giver, but a cheerful giver.**

Ask: What does your face look like when you are cheerful? Show me your cheerful face. *(Wait until all the children are making cheerful smiles.)*

Place a chair in the center of your room.

Say: *(Child's name),* **come sit in the chair and show us your cheerful face.**

Have the child say the Bible verse, "God loves a cheerful giver" (2 Corinthians 9:7), while he or she is sitting in the chair. Give each child a turn.

Fruit of the Spirit Prayers

Supplies

None

Have the children stand in a circle.

Say: Generosity is one of the fruit of the Spirit. When we are generous, we are willing to give to others. We are willing to share. Listen to a poem about the fruit of the Spirit. Say the words of the poem after me and do what I do.

Love, joy, peace
are words that show we care.
So give a hug, *(Hug yourself.)*
laugh out loud, *(Put your hands on your stomach and shake.)*
then say a quiet prayer. *(Fold hands in prayer.)*

Patience, kindness, generosity
remind us what to do.
Wait for our turn, *(Stand still.)*
act with love, *(Point to your heart.)*
and share with others too. *(Move arms out as if presenting a gift.)*

Faithfulness, gentleness, self-control
are three big words to know.
Trust our great God, *(Cross your hands over your heart.)*
use kind words, *(Cup hands around mouth.)*
and choose right as we grow. *(Squat down and then stretch up tall.)*

© 2008 Abingdon Press

Pray: Thank you, God, for helping us be cheerful givers. Thank you for our friends *(name each child and teacher).* **Amen.**

REPRODUCIBLE 6A

God loves a cheerful giver.

2 Corinthians 9:7

REPRODUCIBLE 6B

All-in-One

BIBLE PRESCHOOL

FUN

Faithfulness

Bible Verse

Be faithful to God.

Joshua 22:5, GNT, adapted

Bible Story

Galatians 5:22–23; 2 Kings 22:1–23:5

Galatians 5:22–23 lists faithfulness as the seventh fruit of the Spirit. Meaning "full of faith," faithfulness is evident when a person trusts God completely and makes the commitment to be Christian at any cost. To be faithful, we not only believe in Christ, but we also act on that belief.

The Southern Kingdom of Judah was ruled by the house of David until Judah fell to the Babylonians about 587 B.C. Josiah, who reigned from about 640 to 609 B.C., became king when he was eight years old. Sometime in his twenties, Josiah began to make his own decisions.

Josiah looked around and saw that the worship practices of Assyria had, over time, influenced the worship practices of his people. These worship practices did not reflect what God intended worship to be. Many laws and rituals were ignored and eventually forgotten. Josiah, unlike most of Judah's kings, was faithful to God. Josiah ordered that the Temple at Jerusalem be repaired. During the

restoration of the Temple some form of the Book of Deuteronomy was discovered (probably chapters 12–26 of our present Book of Deuteronomy). Deuteronomy was the book of Jewish law.

Huldah the prophetess verified the authenticity of the scroll, and Josiah called the people together for them to hear the words of the Law and for them to renew their covenant with God. The discovery of this book of Law helped Josiah reform the practices of the Hebrew people. Josiah established the Temple in Jerusalem as the central place of worship and reinstated the celebration of Passover.

Faithfulness to God set Josiah apart from the other kings of Judah and from his own people. Josiah attempted to bring his people back to faithfulness to the God of the covenant, instead of following the general fads of the culture around them.

We can be faithful and do what God wants us to do.

If time is limited, we recommend those activities that are noted in **boldface**. Depending on your time and the number of children, you may be able to include more activities.

ACTIVITY	TIME	SUPPLIES
Crown of Fruit	**10 minutes**	**Reproducible 1A, glue, scissors, crayons or markers, construction paper, tape or stapler and staples**
Hide and Seek	5 minutes	Reproducible 7A, scissors
The Faithful Train	5 minutes	None
Bible Story: A Faithful King	**10 minutes**	**None**
Bible Verse Fun	**10 minutes**	**Bible**
High and Low	10 minutes	Reproducible 7B, tape
Potter's Corner	10 minutes	Reproducible 7B, sandpaper or corrugated cardboard, tape, crayons with papers removed, brown paper bags, scissors
King for a Day	10 minutes	crowns from "Crown of Fruit" activity (Reproducible 1A)
Fruit of the Spirit Prayers	**5 minutes**	**None**

Supplies

Reproducible 1A, glue, scissors, crayons or markers, construction paper, tape or stapler and staples

Crown of Fruit

Photocopy and cut apart the fruit pictures (**Reproducible 1A**) for each child. Cut a piece of construction paper in half lengthwise for each child.

Give each child the construction paper halves. Help each child tape or staple the halves together to make one long strip.

Give each child the fruit pictures. Encourage the children to glue the fruit pictures onto their paper strips. Let the children decorate the fruit pictures with crayons or markers.

Measure the paper strip around each child's head to make a crown. Tape or staple the ends together. If you use staples, be sure that the prongs face out away from the child's head. Encourage the children to wear their crowns.

Say: The fruits on our crowns can help us remember the fruit of the Spirit. God wants us to be faithful. Faithfulness is one of the fruit of the Spirit. When we are faithful, we trust God and do what God wants us to do. We made crowns because our Bible story today is about a king who was faithful. The king found a very important scroll. The scroll told the people how to do what God wanted them to do.

> **We can be faithful
> and do what God wants us to do.**

Supplies

Reproducible 7A, scissors

Hide and Seek

Photocopy and cut apart the bricks and clay jar pictures (**Reproducible 7A**). Show the children the pictures. Place the brick pictures face up on the table or rug. Have the children close their eyes or cover their eyes with their hands. Slide the picture of the clay jar under one of the brick pictures. Have the children open their eyes. Let the children guess where the clay jar is hidden. Continue to play the game as long as the children show interest.

Say: Faithfulness is one of the fruit of the Spirit. When we are faithful, we trust God and do what God wants us to do. Our Bible story today is about a king who was faithful. The king found a very important scroll. The scroll was inside a clay jar. The scroll told the people how to do what God wanted them to do.

The Faithful Train

Supplies

None

Say: Faithfulness is one of the fruit of the Spirit. When we are faithful, we trust God and do what God wants us to do.

We can be faithful and do what God wants us to do.

Lead the children in the following movement activity. Encourage the children to make a train and to move around the room. End the movement in your story area.

Come follow me and make a train.
(Have each child stand behind you to make a train.)
Come follow me right now.
Stretch out your hands
(Have each child touch the shoulders
of the person in front of him or her.)
To make a train.
I'm sure you all know how.

Get on board the faithful train.
(Keep adding children until everyone is participating.)
Get on board right now.
Stretch out your hands
(Have each child touch the shoulders
of the person in front of him or her.)
To make a train.
I'm sure you all know how.

Choo, choo, choo.
Chug, chug, chug.
Around the room we go.
(Shuffle around the room.)

Choo, choo, choo.
Chug, chug, chug.
For faithfulness we can show.
(Shuffle around the room.)

Be faithful. Be faithful.
(Keep repeating.)

A Faithful King

by Daphna Flegal

Have the children sit down on the floor in your story area. Show the children the motions for "Wham! Scrape! Scrape! Wham!" and "Hurray! Hurray!" Have the children do the motions with you as you tell the story.

Say: Our Bible story today is about a king who was faithful. The king's name was Josiah. King Josiah's workmen found a very important scroll. The scroll was inside a clay jar. The scroll told the people how to do what God wanted them to do.

Wham! Scrape! Scrape! Wham!
(Hit floor with your palms; rub palms together twice; hit floor with your palms.)

Wham! Scrape! Scrape! Wham!
(Hit floor with your palms; rub palms together twice; hit floor with your palms.)

King Josiah was a good king. He wanted the people to be faithful to God. So he ordered the workmen to repair the Temple. The Temple was a special place where the people went to worship God.

Wham! Scrape! Scrape! Wham!
(Hit floor with your palms; rub palms together twice; hit floor with your palms.)

Wham! Scrape! Scrape! Wham!
(Hit floor with your palms; rub palms together twice; hit floor with your palms.)

The workmen were hard at work. All at once someone shouted, "Hey!"

The men stopped working.

"Look at the hole in this wall," said one of the workmen. "I see something in there."

"What is it?" asked the other workmen.

"I see a clay jar," answered the man.

Wham! Scrape! Scrape! Wham!
(Hit floor with your palms; rub palms together twice; hit floor with your palms.)

Wham! Scrape! Scrape! Wham!
(Hit floor with your palms; rub palms together twice; hit floor with your palms.)

The men took down part of the wall. They saw a clay jar. They carefully removed the jar from the wall. In the jar was a scroll. God's laws were written on the scroll.

Hurray! Hurray!
(Clap hands.)

The men cheered and shouted. They ran to show the scroll to King Josiah.

Hurray! Hurray!
(Clap hands.)

The king was happy to see the scroll.

"Please read the scroll to me at once!" said King Josiah. "I want to know God's laws so that I can do what God wants me to do."

Bible Verse Fun

Choose a child to hold the Bible open to Joshua 22:5.

Say: Faithfulness is one of the fruit of the Spirit. When we are faithful, we trust God and do what God wants us to do. Our Bible story today is about a king who was faithful. The king found a very important scroll. The scroll told the people how to do what God wanted them to do.

Say the Bible verse, "Be faithful to God" (Joshua 22:5, GNT, adapted), for the children. Have the children say the Bible verse after you.

> ## We can be faithful
> ## and do what God wants us to do.

Help the children learn the Bible verse by singing. Sing the song printed below to the tune of "The Farmer in the Dell."

O, "be faithful to God."
O, "be faithful to God."
The Bible tells us what to do.
so "be faithful to God."

Let the children move to the Bible verse. Have the children stand in a line. Stand at one end of the line yourself. Hand a Bible to the child next to you.

Say: We found a special book.

The child hands the book to the next child and repeats the words and so on down the line.

Move to the other end of the line while the Bible is being passed. When the Bible reaches you, send it back down the line.

Say: It tells us what to do.

Then move to the other end of the line again.

At the other end, reverse direction again.

Say: Be faithful to God.

When the Bible gets to the other end of the line, hold on to it.

Say: The Bible tells us what God wants us to do. God wants us to be faithful to God.

Reproducible
7B, tape

High and Low

Photocopy the clay jar **(Reproducible 7B)**. Follow the directions on the page to make the jar three-dimensional. Show the children the jar.

Say: **Our Bible story today is about a king who was faithful. The king found a very important scroll. The scroll told the people how to do what God wanted them to do. The scroll was inside a clay jar. Let's play a game to find the clay jar. First I will hide the jar. I will hide it high.**

Have the children turn their backs or cover their eyes. Hide the jar somewhere high in the room such as on top of a book shelf. Have the children move around the room on their tiptoes looking for the jar. When someone finds the jar, take it down for them and show it to everyone.

Say: **Now let's hide the jar low.**

Have the children turn their backs or cover their eyes. Hide the jar somewhere low in the room such as underneath a table or chair. Have the children move around the room on their hands and knees looking for the jar. When someone finds the jar, have him or her bring it back to you. Continue the game as long as the children show interest.

Supplies

Reproducible
7B, sandpaper
or corrugated
cardboard,
tape, crayons
with papers
removed,
brown paper
bags, scissors

Potter's Corner

Photocopy the clay jar **(Reproducible 7B)** for each child. Tape a piece of sandpaper or corrugated cardboard to the table. Lightly tape each clay jar picture over the sandpaper or cardboard. Let the children make texture rubbings by rubbing crayons (with papers removed) over their jar pictures. The texture will show through the rubbing.

Help each child fold his or her jar picture in half along the dotted line. Then help each child roll the strip into a tube and tape the edges to make a three-dimensional jar.

Cut a 5-by-7-inch rectangle out of a brown paper bag for each child. Let the children decorate the papers with crayons. Show the children how to roll the papers like a scroll and place them inside their jars.

Say: **King Josiah was faithful. He found a very important scroll. The scroll told the people how to be faithful and how to do what God wanted them to do. The scroll was inside a clay jar.**

King for a Day

Say: Our Bible story today is about a king who was faithful.

Choose a child to be king. Have the child stand up in front of the group. Encourage the child to wear one of the crowns made earlier in the lesson.

Say: King (*child's name*), what can you do?

Help the child think of a motion and then show the motion to the other children. Encourage all the children to do the motion.

Stop moving and **say: King (*child's name*), be faithful to God** (Joshua 22:5, GNT, adapted).

Choose a different child to be king. Continue the game as long as the children show interest.

Fruit of the Spirit Prayers

Have the children stand in a circle.

Say: Today we learned that faithfulness is one of the fruit of the Spirit. When we are faithful, we trust God and do what God wants us to do. Listen to a poem about the fruit of the Spirit. Say the words of the poem after me and do what I do.

Love, joy, peace
are words that show we care.
So give a hug, (*Hug yourself.*)
laugh out loud, (*Put your hands on your stomach and shake.*)
then say a quiet prayer. (*Fold hands in prayer.*)

Patience, kindness, generosity
remind us what to do.
Wait for our turn, (*Stand still.*)
act with love, (*Point to your heart.*)
and share with others too. (*Move arms out as if presenting a gift.*)

Faithfulness, gentleness, self-control
are three big words to know.
Trust our great God, (*Cross your hands over your heart.*)
use kind words, (*Cup hands around mouth.*)
and choose right as we grow. (*Squat down and then stretch up tall.*)

Pray: Thank you, God, for helping us be faithful. Thank you for our friends (*name each child and teacher*). Amen.

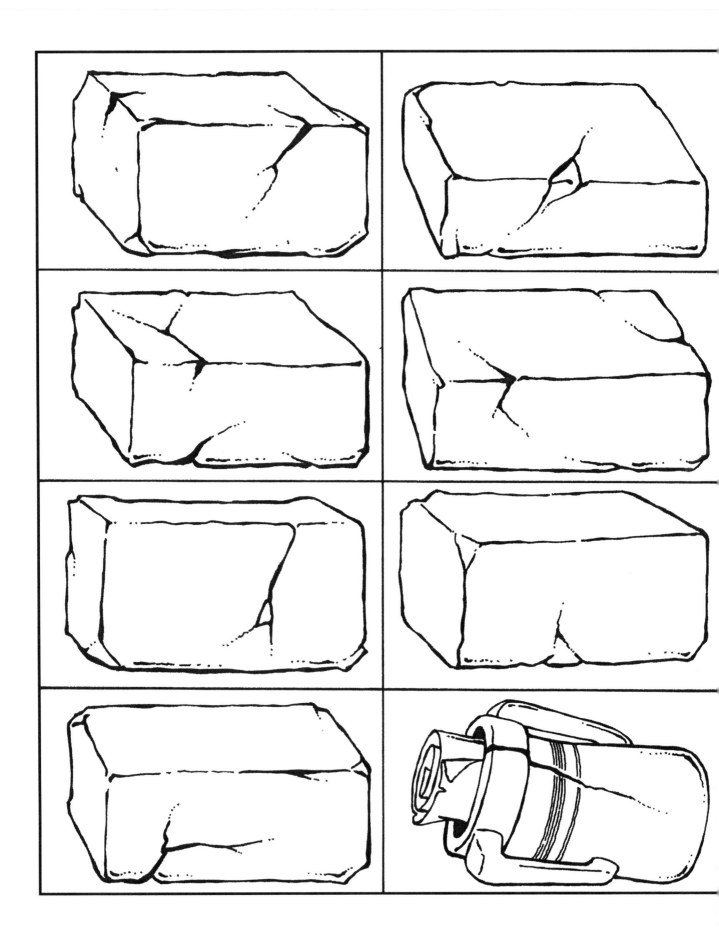

REPRODUCIBLE 7A

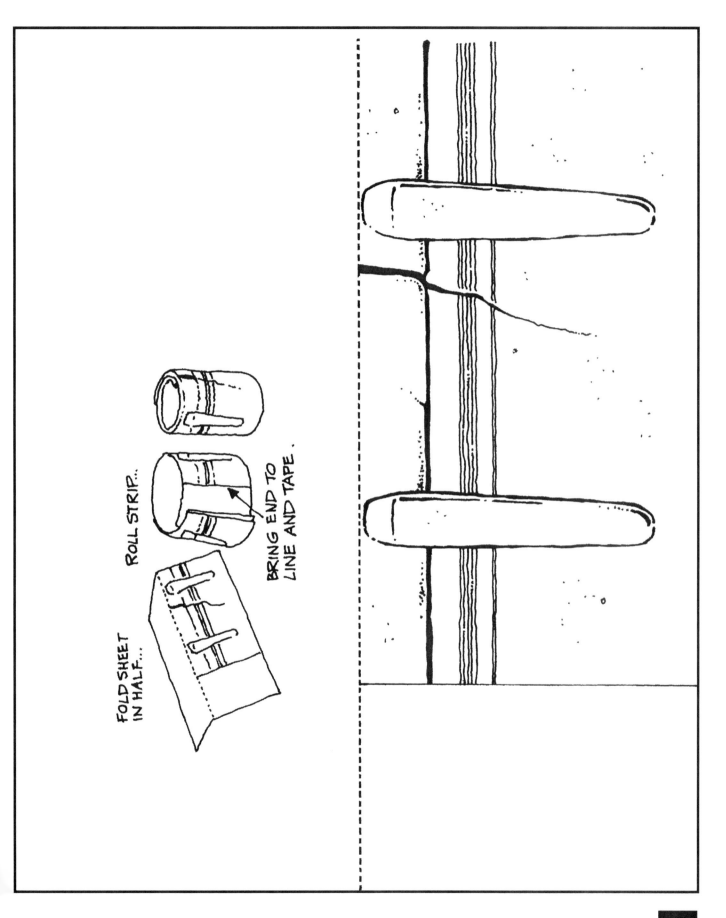

ROLL STRIP...

FOLD SHEET
IN HALF...

BRING END TO
LINE AND TAPE.

REPRODUCIBLE 7B

All-in-One
BIBLE PRESCHOOL
FUN

Gentleness

Bible Verse

Let your gentleness be known to everyone.

Philippians 4:5

Bible Story

Galatians 5:22–23; Psalm 23

Gentleness is the eighth fruit of the Spirit listed in Galatians 5:22–23. Gentleness is deliberate kindness. It is voluntary thoughtfulness that influences our interactions with every person we know and meet. With gentleness come meekness and humility. Being considerate of others, putting away our pride, and focusing on serving others rather than ourselves are manifestations of Christian gentleness.

With almost certainty the Twenty-third Psalm is quoted more than any other Old Testament Scripture passage. It conveys many images and fills our minds with pictures. The first one, "The Lord is my shepherd," immediately brings to mind the One who is responsible for caring for the defenseless.

Sheep need great care. They are easily led astray. They eat things that are not good for them. They do not have a lot of defenses against predatory animals. A shepherd's care gives sheep a much better chance of survival.

In the Twenty-third Psalm we see God as the caretaker, the "shepherd" of God's special "flock of sheep," that is, people. God tries to keep us from going astray; to help us do what is good for ourselves; and to protect us from those things that we do to each other.

In Psalm 23 the images of how God does this demonstrate a gentle, caring, nurturing relationship that God has with God's people. God makes us "lie down in green pastures." (We need rest; God gives us the sabbath.) God leads us in "right paths" (so that we do not end up lost to God). And God walks with us "through the darkest valley." (God is with us even in the bad times.) If we allow God to treat us gently, then God will care for all our needs.

When we treat others lovingly and gently, we are treating them as the Good Shepherd of Psalm 23 treats his sheep, as God treats us. The best way for us to thank God for God's care and gentleness is to treat the rest of God's flock (people) with that same gentleness.

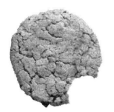

We can be gentle and kind to others.

If time is limited, we recommend those activities that are noted in **boldface**. Depending on your time and the number of children, you may be able to include more activities.

ACTIVITY	TIME	SUPPLIES
Fruity Pillows	**10 minutes**	**Reproducible 1A, crayons or markers, construction paper, stapler and staples, tissue paper or newspaper, glue, tape**
Gentle Thoughts	10 minutes	Reproducible 8A, crayons or markers
The Gentle Train	5 minutes	None
Bible Story: A Gentle Shepherd	**10 minutes**	**pillows from "Fruity Pillows" activity (Reproducible 1A)** **Bible**
Bible Verse Fun	**10 minutes**	
Be Gentle	15 minutes	Reproducible 8B, pennies or metal washers, chenille stems, tape, scissors, basket or box
Gentle Prints	15 minutes	plastic, smocks, large bowl or plastic tub, water, colored tempera paint, dishwashing liquid, drinking straws, construction paper
Thank-You Pass	10 minutes	baby bird from "Be Gentle" activity (Reproducible 8B)
Fruit of the Spirit Prayers	**5 minutes**	**None**

JOIN THE FUN

BIBLE STORY FUN

LIVE THE FUN

Supplies

Reproducible 1A, crayons or markers, construction paper, stapler and staples, tissue paper or newspaper, glue, tape

Fruity Pillows

Photocopy and cut apart the fruit pictures **(Reproducible 1A)** for each child.

Let the children decorate the pictures with crayons or markers. Give each child two pieces of construction paper. Let the children glue their pictures onto one of the construction paper pieces. Place each construction paper with pictures on top of a second piece of construction paper. Staple three of the edges together, leaving one edge open.

Show the children how to crumple tissue paper or newspaper and stuff them into the pillows. Staple the fourth edge together on each pillow. Cover the prongs of the staples with tape. Plan to use the pillows during the Bible Story time.

Say: These fruits can help us remember the fruit of the Spirit. God wants us to be gentle. Gentleness is one of the fruit of the Spirit. When we are gentle, we are kind to one another. Our Bible story today is a psalm. The psalm talks about how a shepherd cares for his sheep.

> ## We can be gentle and kind to others.

Supplies

Reproducible 8A, crayons or markers

Gentle Thoughts

Photocopy the hillside scene **(Reproducible 8A)** for each child. Give each child a picture.

Say: Gentleness is one of the fruit of the Spirit. It is good to be gentle. There are many things in this picture that make us think of gentleness. Can you find them? Find one lamb; three butterflies; two caterpillars; one nest with baby birds; three rabbits; two mice; one frog; one turtle; two ladybugs; three clouds; and five flowers.

Have the children find the items in the pictures. Let the children decorate the pictures with crayons or markers.

Say: Our Bible story today is a psalm. The psalm talks about how a shepherd cares for his sheep.

The Gentle Train

Say: Gentleness is one of the fruit of the Spirit. When we are gentle, we are kind to others.

Supplies

None

We can be gentle and kind to others.

Lead the children in the following movement activity. Encourage the children to make a train and to move around the room. End the movement in your story area.

Come follow me and make a train.
(Have each child stand behind you to make a train.)
Come follow me right now.
Stretch out your hands
*(Have each child touch the shoulders
of the person in front of him or her.)*
To make a train.
I'm sure you all know how.

Get on board the gentle train.
(Keep adding children until everyone is participating.)
Get on board right now.
Stretch out your hands
*(Have each child touch the shoulders
of the person in front of him or her.)*
To make a train.
I'm sure you all know how.

Choo, choo, choo.
Chug, chug, chug.
Around the room we go.
(Shuffle around the room.)

Choo, choo, choo.
Chug, chug, chug.
For gentleness we can show.
(Shuffle around the room.)

Be gentle. Be gentle.
(Keep repeating.)

A Gentle Shepherd

by LeeDell Stickler

Have the children bring their pillows (see page 82) to the story area. Encourage the children to lie down on their pillows. Tell the children the story based on Psalm 23 in a very calm, quiet voice. Have the children quietly repeat, "The LORD is my shepherd."

The LORD is my shepherd, I shall not want.
God gives me good food to eat:
　　cereal and juice;
　　peanut butter and jelly;
　　pizza and hamburgers and spinach.
God gives me a place to live.
God gives me friends and family.

The LORD is my shepherd.

He makes me lie down in green pastures; he leads me beside still waters;
God watches over me
　　when I get up;
　　when I'm at home;
　　when I play with my friends;
　　when I go to sleep at night.

The LORD is my shepherd.

He restores my soul.
God knows my feelings
　　when I'm angry;
　　when I'm sad;
　　when I'm hurt;
And I don't feel so lonely.

The LORD is my shepherd.

He leads me in right paths for his name's sake.
God is like a teacher who helps me
　　be kind to others;
　　remember to say please and thank you;
　　share with others.

The LORD is my shepherd.

Even though I walk through the darkest valley, I fear no evil; for you are with me; your rod and your staff—they comfort me.
God is there in bad times as well as good times:
　　when I'm sick;
　　when I'm afraid;
　　when I don't know what to do.

The LORD is my shepherd.

You prepare a table before me in the presence of my enemies;
God wants me to get along with all people:
　　people I don't like;
　　people who are different from me.

The LORD is my shepherd.

You anoint my head with oil; my cup overflows.
God makes me feel special.
　　And I am special.
　　I am a child of God.
　　God loves me just the way I am.

The LORD is my shepherd.

Surely goodness and mercy shall follow me all the days of my life, and I shall dwell in the house of the LORD my whole life long.
When I think about God,
　　I am happy
　　Because I know
　　God will always love me.

The LORD is my shepherd.

Bible Verse Fun

Choose a child to hold the Bible open to Philippians 4:5.

Say: Gentleness is one of the fruit of the Spirit. When we are gentle, we are kind to one another. Our Bible story today is a psalm. The psalm talks about how a shepherd cares for his sheep.

> ## We can be gentle and kind to others.

Say the Bible verse, "Let your gentleness be known to everyone" (Philippians 4:5), for the children. Have the children say the Bible verse after you.

Help the children learn the Bible verse by singing. Sing the song printed below to the tune of "London Bridge."

> "Let your gentleness be known
> to ev'ryone, to ev'ryone.
> Let your gentleness be known
> to ev'ryone."

Let the children move to the Bible verse.

Say: The shepherd in our Bible story was gentle with the sheep. Let's play a game where the shepherd gently touches a sheep and the sheep has to guess who the shepherd is.

Choose one child to be the sheep and move him or her a little way from the group with his or her back to the group. Silently choose a child from the group to be the shepherd. The group needs to remain quiet.

Have the shepherd tiptoe up behind the sheep and gently touch the sheep on the back. The shepherd says the Bible verse. The sheep then tries to guess who the shepherd is. The sheep may have three guesses.

Whether or not the sheep guesses correctly, both children return to the group. Then choose another sheep and shepherd.

Supplies

Reproducible 8B, pennies or metal washers; chenille stems, tape, scissors, basket or box

Be Gentle

Photocopy the baby bird **(Reproducible 8B)**. Assemble the bird according to the illustration. You may want to make more than one bird if you have a large group of children. Tape a penny or a metal washer to the base of each bird. Place a basket or box on the floor. Place the birds on the floor close to the basket or box.

Make hooks from chenille stems (pipe cleaners). Bend the top three inches of each chenille stem into a hook.

Say: Gentleness is one of the fruit of the Spirit. Whenever I think about caring for someone or something with gentleness, I think about baby birds.

Ask: Have you ever seen a newly hatched baby bird? What is it like? Is it able to care for itself?

Show the children the baby bird.

Say: This baby bird has fallen out of its nest. Pretend you are the mother bird. Use the hook to pick up the bird and put it in the nest. You will need to be very gentle with the baby bird.

Show the children how to hook the baby bird with the chenille stem and put it in the basket or box. Give each child a turn hooking the baby bird and putting it in the basket or box. Compliment the children on how gentle they are being with the bird. Clap and cheer when a bird makes it safely to the nest.

Supplies

plastic, smocks, large bowl or plastic tub, water, colored tempera paint, dishwashing liquid, drinking straws, construction paper

Gentle Prints

Cover the table with plastic. Have the children wear smocks. Place a large bowl or plastic tub partially filled with water on the plastic. Add colored tempera paint to the water. Pour in several squirts of dishwashing liquid.

Give each child a drinking straw. Have the children practice blowing, not sucking, through the straw. Then let the children put their straws into the tub of water and blow. As they blow, bubbles will form.

Give each child a piece of construction paper to make bubble prints. Show the children how to place their papers gently on top of the bubbles to make the prints. Remind the children that they must handle their papers gently to make the bubble prints.

We can be gentle and kind to others.

Thank-You Pass

Supplies

baby bird from "Be Gentle" activity (Reproducible 8B)

Have the children stand in a line, one behind the other.

Say: Gentleness is one of the fruit of the Spirit. When we are gentle, we are kind to one another. What are some ways we can be kind and gentle?

Help the children think of ways we can be kind and gentle, such as sharing toys, taking turns, helping each other, and saying "please" and "thank you."

Say: One way we can be kind to one another is to say, "Thank you." Let's pass the baby bird to one other. When you get the baby bird, say, "Thank you."

Give the first child in line the baby bird. Have the child gently pass the bird to the child behind him or her. Have that child take the bird and say, "Thank you." Continue passing the bird down the line to the last child. Then have the child tiptoe to the front of the line and begin passing the bird again.

Fruit of the Spirit Prayers

Supplies

None

Have the children stand in a circle.

Say: Gentleness is one of the fruit of the Spirit. When we are gentle, we are kind to others. Listen to a poem about the fruit of the Spirit. Say the words of the poem after me and do what I do.

Love, joy, peace
are words that show we care.
So give a hug, *(Hug yourself.)*
laugh out loud, *(Put your hands on your stomach and shake.)*
then say a quiet prayer. *(Fold hands in prayer.)*

Patience, kindness, generosity
remind us what to do.
Wait for our turn, *(Stand still.)*
act with love, *(Point to your heart.)*
and share with others too. *(Move arms out as if presenting a gift.)*

Faithfulness, gentleness, self-control
are three big words to know.
Trust our great God, *(Cross your hands over your heart.)*
use kind words, *(Cup hands around mouth.)*
and choose right as we grow. *(Squat down and then stretch up tall.)*

© 2008 Abingdon Press

Pray: Thank you, God, for helping us be gentle. Thank you for our friends *(name each child and teacher).* Amen.

REPRODUCIBLE 8A

CUT ON SOLID LINE

STAPLE

Self-Control

Bible Verse

Let us choose what is right.

Job 34:4

Bible Story

Galatians 5:22–23; Daniel 1:1–20

Self-control is the last of the fruit of the Spirit listed in Galatians 5:22–23. Self-control is more than moderation; it is the ability to control our actions, feelings, and responses. Having self-control means that we do not give in to our basic instincts; we completely give ourselves to the will of God.

The story of young Daniel is a good example of self-control. The setting for the first chapter of the Book of Daniel is the capture of Jerusalem by King Nebuchadnezzar. The Babylonians took captive a young man by the name of Daniel, whose name means "God is my judge." It appears to have been a custom for some of the young men to have been selected for higher education. This was evidently a great honor and required great mental and physical stamina. These young courtiers would be trained to serve the king.

Daniel and his friends were selected for this type of training. Eating rich foods and wines from the king's table was one of the privileges of this position. Since this was enjoyable, it must have been tempting for the young men to give in to this custom.

However, Daniel and his companions exhibited large amounts of self-control. Daniel and his friends were faithful to God, and they refused to disobey the dietary laws of God.

Since they had no control over how the food was prepared, the young men insisted on eating only vegetables, because that was the only way they could be sure that they were obeying God's dietary laws.

Choosing what is right is not always easy; it is an issue of self-control. Learning to make wise choices is one of the skills of growing up. Children at this age do not have many choices allowed them. But they need to practice whenever possible so that when they are faced with larger, more life affecting choices, they are equipped to evaluate and choose wisely.

We can choose what is right.

If time is limited, we recommend those activities that are noted in **boldface**. Depending on your time and the number of children, you may be able to include more activities.

ACTIVITY	TIME	SUPPLIES	
Fruit Art	10 minutes	Reproducible 1A, scissors, small paper bags, scented markers	**JOIN THE FUN**
Self-control Arm Bands	**10 minutes**	**Reproducible 9A, scissors, crayons or markers, tape**	
The Self-control Train	5 minutes	None	**BIBLE STORY FUN**
Bible Story: Daniel	**10 minutes**	**arm bands from "Self-control Arm Bands" activity**	
Bible Verse Fun	**10 minutes**	**Bible, Reproducibles 9A and 9B, scissors, tape**	
Choose 'n Move	10 minutes	None	
The Don't Laugh Game	5 minutes	None	
Show Me	5 minutes	None	**LIVE THE FUN**
Fruit of the Spirit Prayers	**5 minutes**	**None**	

Supplies

Reproducible 1A, scissors, small paper bags, scented markers

Fruit Art

Photocopy two sets of the fruit pictures page **(Reproducible 1A)** for each child. Cut apart one set of the pictures and place them in a small paper bag for each child. Leave the second set uncut.

Place an uncut page in front of each child. Let the children decorate the pictures with scented markers. Then give each child a paper bag with the cut pictures inside. Have the children shake their bags to mix up the pictures.

Say: These fruits are called the fruit of the Spirit. The first fruit of the Spirit is love. Find the strawberry inside your bag. Your strawberry shows the word *love*.

Have the children find the strawberry and match to the strawberry on their uncut page. Continue naming, finding, and matching all nine of the fruit of the Spirit pictures.

After you match the self-control picture, **say: God wants us to have self-control. Self-control is one of the fruit of the Spirit. Our Bible story today is about a young man named Daniel. Daniel had self-control. He had to make some hard choices about what food to eat. Daniel chose to eat the kinds of foods that God wanted him to eat. These foods were good for him and helped his body be healthy.**

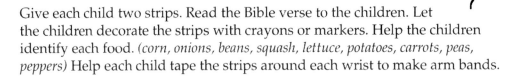

We can choose what is right.

Supplies

Reproducible 9A, scissors, crayons or markers, tape

Self-control Arm Bands

Photocopy and cut apart the Bible verse strips **(Reproducible 9A)** for each child. Save the vegetable pictures to use later.

Give each child two strips. Read the Bible verse to the children. Let the children decorate the strips with crayons or markers. Help the children identify each food. *(corn, onions, beans, squash, lettuce, potatoes, carrots, peas, peppers)* Help each child tape the strips around each wrist to make arm bands.

Say: Self-control is one of the fruit of the Spirit. Self-control is when we make good choices about what we say and do. Our Bible story today is about a young man named Daniel. Daniel had self-control. He had to make some hard choices about what food to eat. Daniel chose to eat the kinds of foods that God wanted him to eat that were good for him and helped his body be healthy. We can choose to eat foods that are good for us like the foods pictured on our arm bands.

The Self-control Train

Say: Self-control is one of the fruit of the Spirit. Self-control is when we make good choices about what we say and do. We choose what is right.

Supplies

None

We can choose what is right.

Lead the children in the following movement activity. Encourage the children to make a train and to move around the room. End the movement in your story area.

Come follow me and make a train.
(Have each child stand behind you to make a train.)
Come follow me right now.
Stretch out your hands
(Have each child touch the shoulders
of the person in front of him or her.)
To make a train.
I'm sure you all know how.

Get on board the self-control train.
(Keep adding children until everyone is participating.)
Get on board right now.
Stretch out your hands
(Have each child touch the shoulders
of the person in front of him or her.)
To make a train.
I'm sure you all know how.

Choo, choo, choo.
Chug, chug, chug.
Around the room we go.
(Shuffle around the room.)

Choo, choo, choo.
Chug, chug, chug.
For self-control we can show.
(Shuffle around the room.)

Have self-control. Have self-control.
(Keep repeating.)

Daniel

by Daphna Flegal

Have the children wear their Self-control Arm Bands **(Reproducible 9A, page 92)** *and sit down in your story area. Each time you say the repeating verse, have the children rub their stomachs and then wave their wrists in the air to show their arm bands.*

(Rub your stomach.)
Round peas and broccoli,
Carrots that crunch,
Green beans and sweet corn,
Let's eat those for lunch.
(Wave your wrists in the air.)

Daniel and his friends lived at the king's palace. The king liked Daniel. He wanted Daniel and his friends to have plenty of good food to eat.

(Rub your stomach.)
Round peas and broccoli,
Carrots that crunch,
Green beans and sweet corn,
Let's eat those for lunch.
(Wave your wrists in the air.)

The king had his servant bring Daniel and his friends food right from the king's table. There was lots of food, but Daniel knew the king's food would not help his body grow healthy and strong.

(Rub your stomach.)
Round peas and broccoli,
Carrots that crunch,
Green beans and sweet corn,
Let's eat those for lunch.
(Wave your wrists in the air.)

Daniel and his friends refused to eat the king's food. The king's servant was afraid he would get into trouble if Daniel and his friends did not eat the king's food.

(Rub your stomach.)
Round peas and broccoli,
Carrots that crunch,
Green beans and sweet corn,
Let's eat those for lunch.
(Wave your wrists in the air.)

Daniel didn't want to get the servant into trouble. He asked the servant to bring him and his friends vegetables to eat and water to drink for ten days.

(Rub your stomach.)
Round peas and broccoli,
Carrots that crunch,
Green beans and sweet corn,
Let's eat those for lunch.
(Wave your wrists in the air.)

The servant agreed. Daniel and his friends ate vegetables and drank water for ten days. When the ten days were up, the servant looked at Daniel and his friends. They looked strong and healthy.

(Rub your stomach.)
Round peas and broccoli,
Carrots that crunch,
Green beans and sweet corn,
Let's eat those for lunch.
(Wave your wrists in the air.)

Daniel and his friends made the right choice. They grew strong and healthy.

Bible Verse Fun

Choose a child to hold the Bible open to Job 34:4.

Say: Self-control is one of the fruit of the Spirit. Our Bible story today is about a young man named Daniel. Daniel had self-control. He had to make some hard choices about what food to eat. Daniel chose to eat the kinds of foods that God wanted him to eat. These foods were good for him and helped his body be healthy.

 We can choose what is right.

Say the Bible verse, "Let us choose what is right" (Job 34:4), for the children. Have the children say the Bible verse after you.

Help the children learn the Bible verse by singing. Sing the song printed below to the tune of "Mary Had a Little Lamb."

Let us cho-ose what is right,
What is right, what is right.
Let us cho-ose what is right,
Let us choose what is right.

Let the children move to the Bible verse. Photocopy and cut apart the vegetable pictures (**Reproducibles 9A and 9B**) so that each child will have one picture. Tape a vegetable picture to each child's clothing. Make sure the child can name the vegetable pictured. There should be more than one child with each vegetable pictured. Have the children stand in a circle.

Say: Self-control is one of the fruit of the Spirit. Our Bible story today is about a young man named Daniel. Daniel had self-control. He had to make some hard choices about what food to eat. Daniel chose to eat the kinds of foods that God wanted him to eat. These foods were good for him and helped his body be healthy.

Ask: What foods did Daniel choose to eat? *(vegetables)*

Say: Each of your pictures shows a vegetable. Let's name each vegetable. *(Say the name of each vegetable pictured.)* **I will call out the name of a vegetable. If I name the vegetable on your picture, change places with another person who has the vegetable on his or her picture. When I say our Bible verse, "Choose what is right," everyone change places.**

Play the game like "Fruit Basket Turnover." Practice once or twice before beginning the game so that the children understand how to play.

Supplies

None

Choose 'n Move

Have the children stand in the center of the room.

Say: **Self-control is when we make good choices about what we say and do. Sometimes we make good choices about what we eat, like Daniel did in our Bible story. Sometimes we make good choices about doing things our parents want us to do. Sometimes we make good choices about how we treat others. Listen to these choices. I will name a choice and point to one side of the room. If you think it is a good choice, move to that side of the room. If it is not a good choice, stay where you are.**

Eat only cake and ice cream for breakfast, lunch, and dinner. *(Children stay in the middle of the room.)*

Go to bed when your parents tell you it's bedtime. *(Children move to the side of the room. Then have the children return to the middle of the room.)*

Push your way to the front of the line. *(Children stay in the middle of the room.)*

Remember to wash your hands before you eat dinner. *(Children move to the side of the room. Then have the children return to the middle of the room.)*

Say a prayer before you go to sleep. *(Children move to the side of the room. Then have the children return to the middle of the room.)*

Knock over a friend's block tower because you want a turn playing with the blocks. *(Children stay in the middle of the room.)*

Play with the trucks while you are waiting for your turn to play with the blocks. *(Children move to the side of the room. Then have the children return to the middle of the room.)*

Supplies

None

The Don't Laugh Game

Say: **Let's play a game where you can practice self-control. Someone will try to make you laugh. You will have to control yourself so you don't laugh.**

Have the children sit in a semicircle. Choose a child to sit or stand in front of the others. Encourage he child to make faces and act silly in order to get the others to laugh. Remind the others that they are to use self-control by trying not to laugh.

Choose different children to be silly. Take giggle breaks so everyone can laugh.

Show Me

Supplies

None

Say: Self-control is one of the fruit of the Spirit. Self-control is when we make good choices about what we say and do. Our Bible story today is about a young man named Daniel. Daniel had self-control. He had to make some hard choices about what food to eat. Daniel chose to eat foods that were good for him and helped his body be healthy.

Ask: What are some other things we can choose to do that help our bodies be healthy? (*Brush our teeth, get enough sleep, exercise, not smoke, and so forth.*)

Say: God plans for us to have healthy bodies. We need to make good choices to help keep our bodies healthy. Show me how you brush your teeth. (*Have the children pretend to brush their teeth.*) Show me how you go to sleep. (*Have children pretend to sleep.*) Show me how you exercise. (*Have the children pretend to exercise.*) Very good. When we make good choices, we have self-control.

Fruit of the Spirit Prayers

Supplies

None

Have the children stand in a circle.

Say: Today we learned that self-control is one of the fruit of the Spirit. When we have self-control, we make good choices.

Love, joy, peace
are words that show we care.
So give a hug, (*Hug yourself.*)
laugh out loud, (*Put your hands on your stomach and shake.*)
then say a quiet prayer. (*Fold hands in prayer.*)

Patience, kindness, generosity
remind us what to do.
Wait for our turn, (*Stand still.*)
act with love, (*Point to your heart.*)
and share with others too. (*Move arms out as if presenting a gift.*)

Faithfulness, gentleness, self-control
are three big words to know.
Trust our great God, (*Cross your hands over your heart.*)
use kind words, (*Cup hands around mouth.*)
and choose right as we grow. (*Squat down and then stretch up tall.*)

© 2008 Abingdon Press

Pray: Thank you, God, for helping us have self-control. Thank you for our friends (*name each child and teacher*). Amen.

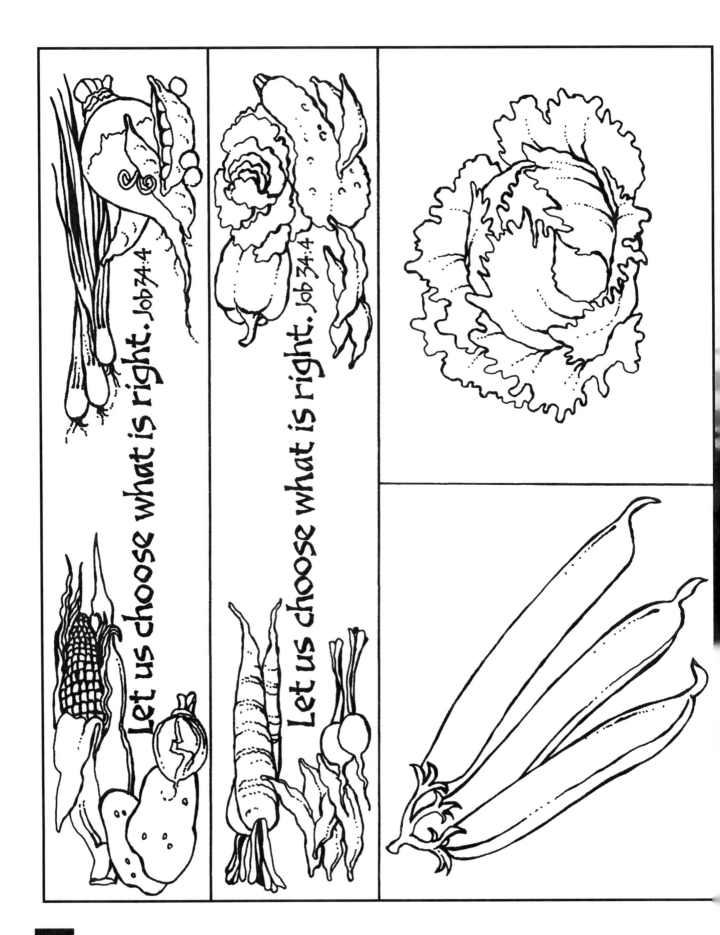

Let us choose what is right. Job 34:4

Let us choose what is right. Job 34:4

REPRODUCIBLE 9A

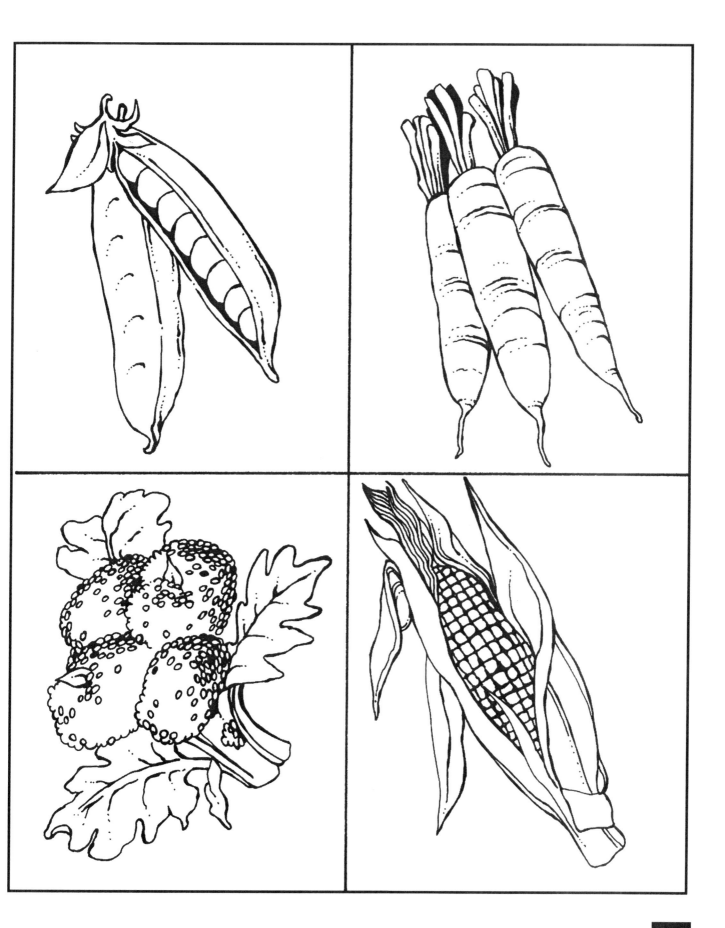

REPRODUCIBLE 9B

All-in-One
BIBLE PRESCHOOL
FUN

Honesty

Bible Verse

Be honest.

Proverbs 14:2, GNT

Bible Story

Luke 19:1–10

Today's lesson talks about the Christian virtue, honesty. To be characterized as an honest person, we must be trustworthy and concerned with the rights of others. The story of Zacchaeus is a good example of honesty.

The story of Zacchaeus is found only in the Book of Luke. Zacchaeus was the chief tax collector in Jericho. It seems that Zacchaeus had amassed a fortune in dishonest revenue from his tax collecting practices. A tax collector was required to collect a set amount of tax for Rome. Anything else the tax collector acquired he could keep. Evidently, Zacchaeus was good at his job—which meant that he made his money by somehow misrepresenting the amount owed or by that old-fashioned method of overcharging.

We do not know if Zacchaeus' conscience bothered him or not. What we do know is that he heard about Jesus and really wanted to see him. However, Zacchaeus was a very short man and could not see over the

crowds, so he climbed a sycamore tree. He not only saw Jesus, but Jesus saw him. Though it was an unpopular decision, Jesus went with Zacchaeus to spend some time in his home.

Jesus had a profound effect on the life of Zacchaeus. The Bible does not tell us that Jesus lectured Zacchaeus. It does tell us that Zacchaeus changed. He did not give up his job as a tax collector, but he did change his business practices. He decided to divide his possessions and give half to the poor. He decided that those he had defrauded should be repaid four times what he had taken from them.

One can only assume that having put this much of a penalty for his dishonesty upon himself, Zacchaeus turned his life into that of an honest man from there on out.

Jesus blessed Zacchaeus and his newfound honesty. This honesty was rewarded by Zacchaeus truly finding God.

We can be honest.

If time is limited, we recommend those activities that are noted in **boldface**. Depending on your time and the number of children, you may be able to include more activities.

ACTIVITY	TIME	SUPPLIES	
Sort It Out	5 minutes	Reproducible 10A, plastic coins	JOIN THE FUN
Hop 'n Hunt	15 minutes	Reproducible 10B; crayons or markers; glue, tape or stapler and staples; plastic coins	
Around the Room	5 minutes	None	BIBLE STORY FUN
Bible Story: An Honest Man	10 minutes	coin bags from "Hop 'n Hunt" activity (Reproducible 10B), plastic coins	
Bible Verse Fun	10 minutes	Bible	
Be Honest	10 minutes	None	
If You're Honest	5 minutes	None	LIVE THE FUN
Guess Who Prayers	5 minutes	None	

Join the Fun

Supplies

Reproducible 10A, plastic coins

Sort It Out

Photocopy several copies of the bags of coins **(Reproducible 10A)**. Place a pile of plastic coins on the table. Let the children match the coins to the coins on the money bags pictures. The children may also sort the money bags according to the number of coins pictured.

Say: The Bible teaches us to be honest. Our Bible story today is about a man named Zacchaeus. Zacchaeus was not honest. He took money that did not belong to him. Then Zacchaeus met someone who helped Zacchaeus change and become an honest man.

> **We can be honest.**

Supplies

Reproducible 10B; crayons or markers; glue, tape, or stapler and staples; plastic coins

Hop 'n Hunt

Before class hide the plastic coins all around your room. Photocopy the coin bags **(Reproducible 10B)** for each child. (You do not need to cut out the bags.)

Let the children decorate the bags with crayons or markers. Show the children how to fold the bags along the dotted lines. Have the children glue, tape, or staple the sides of the bags together to make an envelope. Write the children's names on their coin bags.

Let the children go around the room and hunt for coins. When a child finds a coin, have him or her put it in the bag.

If you wish to make the hunt more active, vary how you have the children move. For instance, tell the children they must hop around the room to hunt for coins. After a few moments of hopping, have the children stop. Then tell the children to crawl around the room to hunt for coins.

When the hunt is finished, have the children place their coin bags in the story area.

Say: The Bible teaches us to be honest. Our Bible story today is about a man named Zacchaeus. Zacchaeus was not honest. He took money that did not belong to him. Then Zacchaeus met someone who helped Zacchaeus change and become an honest man.

Around the Room

Lead the children to your story area with the following movement poem.

Supplies

None

Here we go a-marching,
(March around the room.)
A-marching, a-marching.
Here we go a-marching
all around the room.

Who do we see marching,
(March around the room.)
Marching, marching?
Who do we see marching
All around the room?

We see *(name each child).*
(Stop moving.)

Here we go a-hopping,
(Hop around the room.)
A-hopping, a-hopping.
Here we go a-hopping
all around the room.

Who do we see hopping,
(Hop around the room.)
Hopping, hopping?
Who do we see hopping
All around the room?

We see *(name each child).*
(Stop moving.)

Here we go a-sitting,
(Sit down in your story area.)
A-sitting, a-sitting.
Here we go a-sitting
right here in the room.

Who do we see sitting,
(Sit down in your story area.)
Sitting, sitting?
Who do we see sitting
Right here in the room?

We see *(name each child).*

An Honest Man

by Daphna Flegal

Have the children bring their coin bags from the "Hop n' Hunt" activity (Reproducible 10B) and join you in the story area. Make sure that each child has at least four coins in his or her coin bag. Tell the story as if you were Zacchaeus, or ask another adult to dress up as Zacchaeus and tell the story. Zacchaeus needs to have at least four coins to count at the beginning of the story, as well as extra coins to give back to the children at the end of the story. Zacchaeus goes to each child and takes four of his or her coins when it is indicated in the story. At the end of the story Zacchaeus goes to each child and gives back five coins.

My name is Zacchaeus. No one likes me. I don't have any friends. Do you know why? I'm a tax collector. I take money from people and give it to the Romans. But that's not all. I take more money than I should. Then I keep the extra money for myself. First I take coins for the Romans.

1, 2 for Rome.
(Count coins.)

Then I take coins for me!

1, 2 for me!
(Count coins.)

I know that is not honest, but I don't care! I see you have some coins. Have you paid your taxes?

1, 2 for Rome.
(Take two coins from each child.)

1, 2 for me!
(Take two more coins from each child.)

One day I heard that Jesus was coming to town. Crowds of people hurried into town to see him. I tried to see him, but there were too many people. I decided to climb a tree so that I could see.

Soon I saw Jesus. He smiled and waved to all the people. Then he walked right up to my tree.

He looked up and said, "Zacchaeus, hurry and come down, for I must stay at your house today."

I was so surprised I almost fell climbing down the tree! I took Jesus to my house. He told me all about God. I listened to what Jesus said and decided right then to change my life.

I decided to give back all the money I had taken from the people. I even gave more than I had taken. I decided to be an honest man.

1, 2, 3, 4, 5 for you!
(Give five coins back to each child.)

Bible Verse Fun

Choose a child to hold the Bible open to Proverbs 14:2.

Say: The Bible teaches us to be honest. Our Bible story today is about a man named Zacchaeus. Zacchaeus was not honest. He took money that did not belong to him. Then Zacchaeus met Jesus. Jesus helped Zacchaeus change and become an honest man.

We can be honest.

Say the Bible verse, "Be honest" (Proverbs 14:2, GNT), for the children. Have the children say the Bible verse after you.

Help the children learn the Bible verse by singing. Sing the words printed below to the tune of "Mary Had a Little Lamb."

> The Bible says to "be honest,
> Be honest, be honest."
> The Bible says to "be honest,"
> and that's just what we'll be.

Let the children move to the Bible verse. Have the children stand in a circle.

Say: In our Bible story today a man named Zacchaeus climbed a tree to see Jesus.

Show the children how to pretend to climb a tree by alternating raising your right and left hand and grasping as though grabbing for branches.

Say: Jesus told Zacchaeus to come down from the tree. When we come down from a tree, sometimes we have to jump down from the lowest branch. Let's all jump right now. Zacchaeus came down from the tree and listened to Jesus. Zacchaeus became an honest man.

Have the children practice jumping.

Say: When I say "up a tree" pretend to climb up. When I say "down a tree" jump in place. If I say our Bible verse, "Be honest" everyone sit down on the floor.

Repeat the different phrases several times. Vary the order of the phrases. End the game by saying the Bible verse.

Supplies

None

Be Honest

Say: The Bible teaches us to be honest. Our Bible story today is about a man named Zacchaeus. Zacchaeus was not honest. He took money that did not belong to him. Then Zacchaeus met Jesus. Jesus helped Zacchaeus change and become an honest man.

Say: Listen to these short stories. If the boy or girl is honest, shout out the Bible verse, "Be honest" (Proverbs 14:2, GNT). If the boy or girl is not honest, shake your head and say, "Oh, no!"

Use these statements:

Amy was running through the house. She ran into a table and knocked over a lamp. The lamp broke. Amy told her father that she was the one who broke the lamp. *(Be honest.)*

Amy was running through the house. She ran into a table and knocked over a lamp. The lamp broke. Amy told her father that her brother was the one who broke the lamp. *(Oh, no!)*

Kyle's mother baked some cookies. She told Kyle and his sister not to eat any before supper. The telephone rang, and Mother started talking on the phone. Kyle ate a cookie while Mother wasn't looking. When Kyle's mother got off the phone, she noticed a cookie was missing. She asked Kyle and his sister who had eaten the cookie. Kyle told his mother his sister was the one who had eaten the cookie. *(Oh, no!)*

Kyle's mother baked some cookies. She told Kyle and his sister not to eat any before supper. The telephone rang, and Mother started talking on the phone. Kyle ate a cookie while Mother wasn't looking. When Kyle's mother got off the phone, she noticed a cookie was missing. She asked Kyle and his sister who had eaten the cookie. Kyle told his mother he was the one who had eaten the cookie. *(Be honest.)*

Mark and Lily played outside all morning. When they came in the house, they were suppose to take off their shoes so they would not get dirt in the house, but they forgot. Their shoes left a dirty mess on the floor. When Mother saw the dirt she wanted to know who had made the mess. Mark and Lily said they didn't know who had made the mess. *(Oh, no!)*

Mark and Lily played outside all morning. When they came in the house, they were suppose to take off their shoes so they would not get dirt in the house, but they forgot. Their shoes left a dirty mess on the floor. When Mother saw the dirt she wanted to know who had made the mess. Mark and Lily told Mother that they had made the mess because they had forgotten to take of their shoes. Then they helped Mother sweep up the dirt. *(Be honest.)*

If You're Honest

Say: The Bible teaches us to be honest. Our Bible story today is about a man named Zacchaeus. Jesus helped Zacchaeus become an honest man.

We can be honest.

Sing the song printed below to the tune of "If You're Happy and You Know It." Do the suggested motions.

If you're honest and you know it, clap your hands. *(clap, clap)*
If you're honest and you know it, clap your hands. *(clap, clap)*
If you're honest and you know it, then your face will surely show it.
If you're honest and you know it, clap your hands. *(clap, clap)*

If you're honest and you know it, hop two times. *(hop, hop)*
If you're honest and you know it, hop two times. *(hop, hop)*
If you're honest and you know it, then your face will surely show it.
If you're honest and you know it, hop two times. *(hop, hop)*

If you're honest and you know it, turn around. *(turn around)*
If you're honest and you know it, turn around. *(turn around)*
If you're honest and you know it, then your face will surely show it.
If you're honest and you know it, turn around. *(turn around)*

Guess Who Prayers

Have the children sit in a circle on the floor.

Say: I'm thinking of a friend in our circle. Can you guess who?
(Describe one child until the other children guess the child's name.)

Have the child stand up.

Pray: *(Child's name)* can be honest. Thank you, God, for *(child's name)*.
Amen.

Continue until you have described each child and yourself.

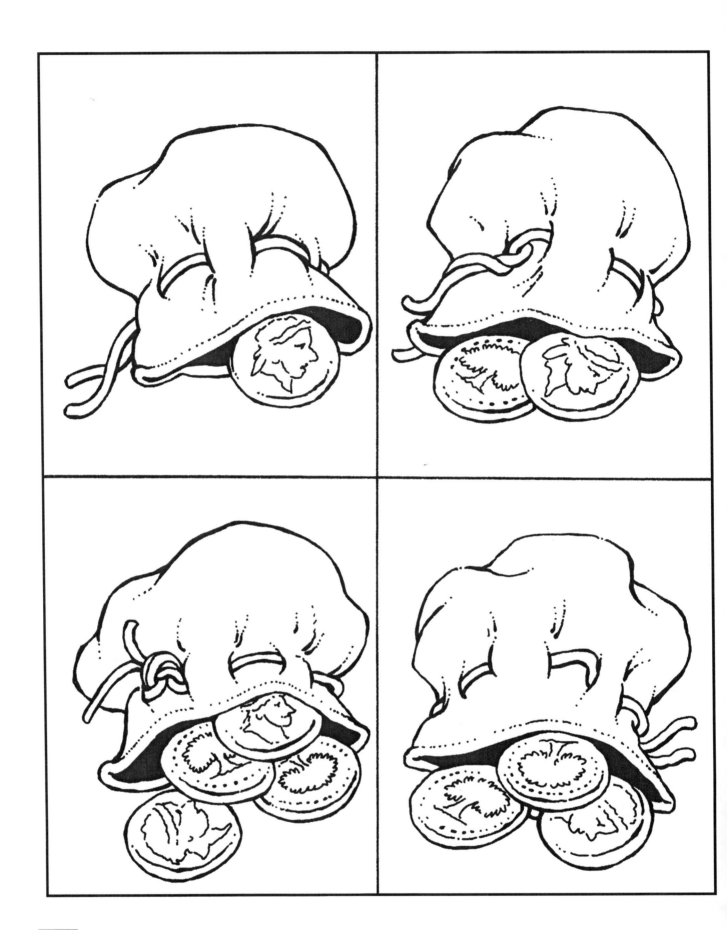

REPRODUCIBLE **10A**

ALL–IN–ONE BIBLE FUN

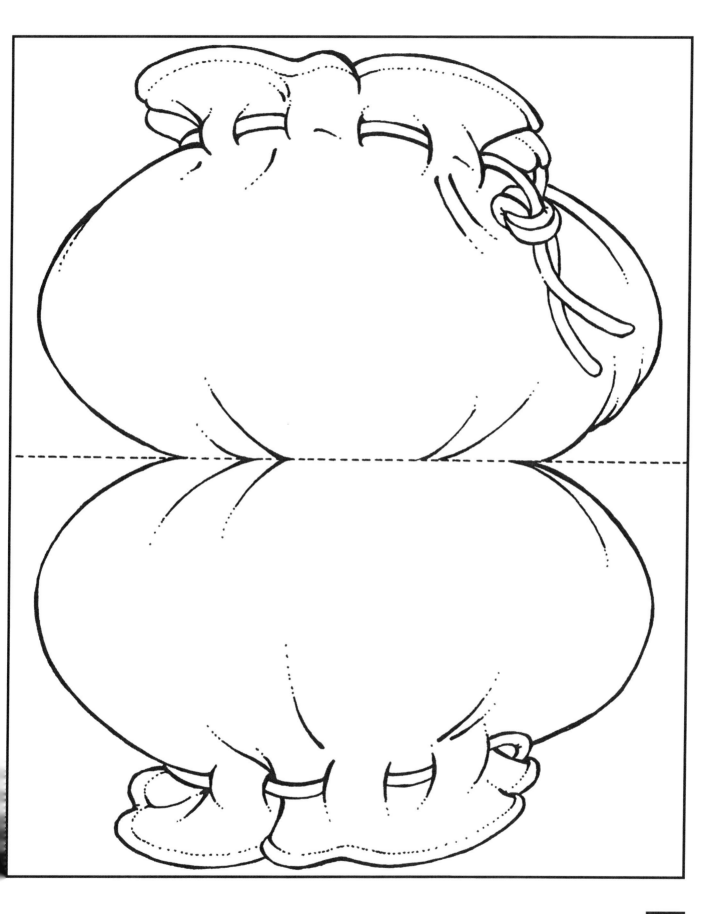

REPRODUCIBLE 10B

All-in-One

BIBLE PRESCHOOL

FUN

Forgiveness

Bible Verse

Forgive one another.

Ephesians 4:32, GNT

Bible Story

Matthew 18:21–35

Forgiveness is another Christian virtue we strive to have. God has forgiven us our sins. As children of God, we are called to imitate God's tolerance, patience, and forgiveness.

In the time of Jesus, Jewish law stated that forgiving someone three times was sufficient. Even today that seems reasonable. When Peter questions Jesus about how often he should forgive someone, Peter himself suggests a generous seven times. For Jesus, however, even this is not enough. Jesus says we must forgive seventy-seven times, which means infinitely. God's forgiveness requires that our forgiveness of others be limitless.

Jesus illustrates his point about the importance of forgiveness by comparing the kingdom of heaven to a king who wished to be repaid a debt from his servant. The servant owed the king a substantial amount of money. The king, however, generously forgave the servant the entire debt.

Immediately following this, the forgiven servant was asked to forgive a much smaller debt owed him by a fellow servant. But instead of forgiving and being generous, this unforgiving servant refused to forgive this small debt. The unforgiving servant not only demanded payment of the debt but had his poor fellow servant thrown into prison.

When the king learned of this callous behavior on the part of the servant he had forgiven, the king rebuked the servant. The king then had the unforgiving servant treated even more harshly than the servant had treated his fellow servant.

By telling this story, Jesus wanted people to understand that if we expect God to forgive us, we must offer forgiveness to one another.

Young children are just learning to verbalize their feelings. Help them by practicing using the words, "I'm sorry" and "I forgive you."

We can forgive one another.

If time is limited, we recommend those activities that are noted in **boldface**. Depending on your time and the number of children, you may be able to include more activities.

ACTIVITY	TIME	SUPPLIES
Flags, Flags, Flags	**10 minutes**	**Reproducible 11A, crayons or markers, paper punch, yarn, scissors**
Walk 'n Wave	10 minutes	flags (Reproducible 11A), drum or table top
Around the Room	5 minutes	None
Bible Story: Forgive, Forgive	**10 minutes**	**flags from "Flags, Flags, Flags" activity (Reproducible 11A)**
Bible Verse Fun	**10 minutes**	**Bible, optional: CD of Christian music, CD player**
Unlikely Hugs	10 minutes	Reproducible 11B, scissors, crayons or markers, glue
Cat and Mouse	10 minutes	None
Find the Flag	10 minutes	flag from "Flags, Flags, Flags," activity (Reproducible 11A)
Guess Who Prayers	**5 minutes**	**None**

JOIN THE FUN

BIBLE STORY FUN

LIVE THE FUN

JOIN THE FUN

Supplies

Reproducible 11A, crayons or markers, paper punch, yarn, scissors

Flags, Flags, Flags

Let the children make flags to use during today's Bible story. Photocopy the Bible verse and American Sign Language page **(Reproducible 11A)** for each child. Show the children the signs from American Sign Language for "forgive one another."

Have the children decorate the pages with crayons or markers. Show the children how to fold their pages along the dotted lines. Use a paper punch to make two holes along the left-hand side of each page. Help the children tie loops of yarn through the holes to make handles. Show the children how to hold the loops of yarn and wave the flags in the air.

Say: Our Bible tells us to forgive one another. Today our Bible story is a story Jesus told to help people understand about forgiving one another.

We can forgive one another.

Walk 'n Wave

Have the children hold their flags made previously **(Reproducible 11A)** and stand in a circle. Use a drum if you have one available. If not, slap your hands on a table top to make the sounds of a drum.

Supplies

flags (Reproducible 11A), drum or table top

Say: The Bible tells us to forgive one another. When you hear me beat the drum, walk around the circle. When I stop beating the drum, stop walking and listen to me. Each time I say, "Forgive one another," wave your flags.

Beat the drum and have the children walk around the circle. Stop beating the drum and read one of these statements. Have the children respond by waving their flags. Then beat the drum again and have the children walk. Continue until you have read all the statements.

When someone steps on your toe, forgive one another. *(Wave flags.)*
When someone breaks one of your toys, forgive one another. *(Wave flags.)*
When someone knocks over the tower you made out of the blocks,
   forgive one another. *(Wave flags.)*
When someone grabs the toy truck out of your hands, forgive one another.
   (Wave flags.)

Around the Room

Lead the children to your story area with the following movement poem.

Supplies

None

Here we go a-marching,
(March around the room.)
A-marching, a-marching.
Here we go a-marching
all around the room.

Who do we see marching,
(March around the room.)
Marching, marching?
Who do we see marching
All around the room?

We see *(name each child).*
(Stop moving.)

Here we go a-hopping,
(Hop around the room.)
A-hopping, a-hopping.
Here we go a-hopping
all around the room.

Who do we see hopping,
(Hop around the room.)
Hopping, hopping?
Who do we see hopping
All around the room?

We see *(name each child).*
(Stop moving.)

Here we go a-sitting,
(Sit down in your story area.)
A-sitting, a-sitting.
Here we go a-sitting
right here in the room.

Who do we see sitting,
(Sit down in your story area.)
Sitting, sitting?
Who do we see sitting
Right here in the room?

We see *(name each child).*

Forgive, Forgive

by Daphna Flegal

Have the children bring their flags **(Reproducible 11A)** *and join you in the story area.*
Tell the children the story. Each time you say the refrain, have the children wave their flags.

There once was a king
Who lived long ago.
He was a fair king
As this story will show.

Forgive,
Forgive,
Forgive one another.

He called a servant
Who owed him money.
"You must pay me now,
Or it won't be funny."

Forgive,
Forgive,
Forgive one another.

"Please forgive me;
I need more time."
The servant promised
He'd pay every dime.

Forgive,
Forgive,
Forgive one another.

"I will forgive you,"
Said the king so kind.
And the servant left
Before he changed his mind.

Forgive,
Forgive,
Forgive one another.

But as the servant
Went out the door,
He saw a man
He'd met before.

Forgive,
Forgive,
Forgive one another.

"You owe me money,"
Said the servant to the man.
"Pay me right now,
Pay me all you can."

Forgive,
Forgive,
Forgive one another.

"Please forgive me;
I need more time."
The man gave his promise
To pay every dime.

Forgive,
Forgive,
Forgive one another.

"I will not forgive you,"
Said the servant unkind.
"You'll go to jail
'Til the money is mine."

Forgive,
Forgive,
Forgive one another.

The king found out
What the servant had done,
And what happened next
Was not much fun.

Forgive,
Forgive,
Forgive one another.

"I forgave you,"
Said the king that day.
"But you did not forgive,
So now you'll pay."

Forgive,
Forgive,
Forgive one another.

Jesus told this story
About how to live
To teach us all
We should forgive.

Forgive,
Forgive,
Forgive one another.

Bible Verse Fun

Choose a child to hold the Bible open to Ephesians 4:32.

Say: The Bible teaches us to forgive one another.

We can forgive one another.

Say the Bible verse, "Forgive one another" (Ephesians 4:32, GNT), for the children. Have the children say the Bible verse after you.

Help the children learn the Bible verse by singing. Sing the words printed below to the tune of "London Bridge."

The Bible tells us to forgive,
To forgive, to forgive.
The Bible tells us to forgive,
"Forgive one another."

© 1998 Abingdon Press

Let the children move to the Bible verse. Have the children move to an open area of the room.

Sing the Bible verse song again and encourage the children to move about the room. Stop singing. Have the children freeze wherever they are.

Have the children find the person closest to them. Have the children hug that person and say, "Forgive one another." If the children do not wish to hug each other, have them shake hands with each other.

Sing the song again and repeat the game, stopping at a different part of the song. Play the game as long as the children show interest.

If you are uncomfortable singing by yourself, play music from a Christian CD.

Unlikely Hugs

Photocopy the cat and mouse card (**Reproducible 11B**) for each child.

Cut the Bible verse from the bottom of the card. Cut along the solid lines around the cat and mouse.

Give each child a cat and mouse card. Let the children decorate the cards with crayons or markers.

Have the children turn the cards so that the cat and mouse are face down on the table. Let the children glue the Bible verse strips onto the blank sides of the cards. Read the Bible verse to the children.

Show each child how to fold the card so that the cat and mouse look like they are hugging each other.

Say: Our Bible tells us to forgive one another. You can give this card to someone to remind that person that we should forgive one another.

> **We can forgive one another.**

Cat and Mouse

Have the children sit in a circle on the floor.

Say: Let's pretend to be cats and mice. The cats will ask the mice to forgive.

Select one child to be the cat and move to the center of the circle. All the children sitting in the circle will be the mice. Have the cat kneel in front of one of the mice in the circle (in any order at all).

Have the cat say: "Meow, meow! Please forgive me!" Have the mouse pat the cat on the head, and say, "Squeak, squeak! I forgive you."

Then have the cat chase the mouse around the circle. If the cat tags the mouse before he or she can sit back down in the circle, the mouse becomes the new cat. Continue until everyone has had an opportunity to be the cat.

Find the Flag

Show the children the sign language for "forgive one another" from their flags **(Reproducible 11A)**.

Choose a child to be "IT." Have IT hide his or her eyes or step out of the room with a teacher. Hide one of the flags somewhere in the room. Have IT uncover his or her eyes or return to the room.

Say: One of our flags is missing. Can you find it? Look all around the room. If you are getting close to the flag we will all clap for you. If you are getting farther away from the flag we will all say, "I'm sorry."

Have IT look for the flag. Encourage the other children to clap when IT gets close to the flag and say "I'm sorry" when IT goes away from the flag. When IT finds the flag have all the children repeat the Bible verse and do the signs.

Play the game until each child has an opportunity to be IT.

We can forgive one another.

Guess Who Prayers

Have the children sit in a circle on the floor.

Say: I'm thinking of a friend in our circle. Can you guess who? *(Describe one child until the other children guess the child's name.)*

Have the child stand up.

Pray: *(Child's name)* **can forgive. Thank you, God, for** *(child's name).* **Amen.**

Continue until you have described each child and yourself.

Forgive one another.

Ephesians 4:32, Good News Bible

one another

forgive

REPRODUCIBLE 11A

Forgive one another.

Ephesians 4:32, Good News Bible

Obedience

Bible Verse

Children, obey your parents.

Ephesians 6:1

Bible Story

Matthew 24:45–47

Obedience to God is a Christian virtue we strive for. The Ten Commandments offer the framework of our obedience. Obedience to God is not just adhering to the law when we have to or when we are being watched. Obedience is living as a Christian who respects and follows God's laws at all times and in all places.

In this passage from Matthew, Jesus explains the responsibilities of obedience to God. Jesus tells us of how a faithful servant who has been put in charge of his fellow servants should be found doing his tasks when the master returns. If the servant sees that his master is delayed and takes advantage of the situation to disobey his master and mistreat his fellow servants, then that servant will be severely punished.

In this Bible passage Jesus is talking about the Second Coming and about the need for watchfulness and obedience. We do not know the time or the hour. We do not know what God's schedule will be.

Because we are never sure when we are to be called to account for our actions, Jesus tells us that we must be obedient to the wishes of God at all times. We are never to become complacent and lapse into following our own wishes. To be obedient to God only when we think that someone is watching is not enough. To be obedient only when it is useful to us is not enough. We must be obedient to the will of God at all times.

We are to live our lives at all times as God has required of us, by living each day as if God will show up at any moment.

This obedience is not a call to just a set of rules and regulations, but to the heart and spirit of the Gospel, to loving God, and therefore to caring for those whom God loves.

We can obey God, and we can obey our parents.

If time is limited, we recommend those activities that are noted in **boldface**. Depending on your time and the number of children, you may be able to include more activities.

ACTIVITY	TIME	SUPPLIES
Storybook Stop	**10 minutes**	Reproducible 12A, crayons or markers, scissors
Obey Simon	10 minutes	None
Around the Room	5 minutes	None
Bible Story: The Wise Servant	**10 minutes**	storybooks from "Storybook Stop" (Reproducible 12A)
Bible Verse Fun	**10 minutes**	Bible; drum, set of rhythm sticks, blocks, or unsharpened pencils
Promises, Promises	15 minutes	Reproducible 12B, watercolor markers or watercolor paints and paintbrushes, permanent marker or pen
Yes!	5 minutes	None
Tell Us What to Do	10 minutes	None
Guess Who Prayers	**5 minutes**	None

JOIN THE FUN

BIBLE STORY FUN

LIVE THE FUN

Storybook Stop

Supplies

Reproducible 12A, crayons or markers, scissors

Photocopy the story page **(Reproducible 12A)** for each child. Cut out the cards on the solid lines.

Show each child how to fold the page along the dotted lines like a greeting card. Let the children decorate the storybooks with crayons or markers.

Say: Our Bible tells us to obey God and our parents. Today our Bible story is a story Jesus told to help people understand how to obey God. We will read our storybooks when we hear the Bible story.

> **We can obey God,
> and we can obey our parents.**

Write each child's name on his or her storybook. Place the storybooks in your story area.

Obey Simon

Supplies

None

Have the children move to an open area of the room. Play "Simon Says" with the children.

Say: Let's play "Simon Says." In this game you must obey Simon and do what Simon tells you to do. Only move when I say, "Simon says." If I do not say, "Simon says," don't do the motion.

Use the suggestions below to play the game with the children. Do not make the game a competition. Let everyone stay in for the whole game. When the children make a mistake, say something like, "Uh-oh, some of us didn't obey Simon. Let's try again."

Simon says put your hands on your head.
Simon says touch your toes.
Touch your knees. *(Don't move.)*
Simon says shake your hands.
Simon says hop up and down.
Simon says touch your nose.
Touch your elbow. *(Don't move.)*
Touch your ears. *(Don't move.)*
Simon says wiggle your whole body.
Simon says sit down.

Around the Room

Lead the children to your story area with the following movement poem.

Here we go a-marching,
(March around the room.)
A-marching, a-marching.
Here we go a-marching
all around the room.

Who do we see marching,
(March around the room.)
Marching, marching?
Who do we see marching
All around the room?

We see *(name each child)*.
(Stop moving.)

Here we go a-hopping,
(Hop around the room.)
A-hopping, a-hopping.
Here we go a-hopping
all around the room.

Who do we see hopping,
(Hop around the room.)
Hopping, hopping?
Who do we see hopping
All around the room?

We see *(name each child)*.
(Stop moving.)

Here we go a-sitting,
(Sit down in your story area.)
A-sitting, a-sitting.
Here we go a-sitting
right here in the room.

Who do we see sitting,
(Sit down in your story area.)
Sitting, sitting?
Who do we see sitting
Right here in the room?

We see *(name each child)*.

The Wise Servant

by Daphna Flegal and LeeDell Stickler

*Give each child his or her storybook from "Storybook Stop" activity (**Reproducible 12A**). Have the children turn to page 1 of their books.*

Turn to page 1
Jesus told a story about a wise servant.

The servant said:
I am a faithful servant,
As wise as wise can be.
I do just what my master says
Even when he cannot see.

Turn to page 2
The master gave the servant things to do for him while the master was away.

The servant said:
I am a faithful servant,
As wise as wise can be.
I do just what my master says
Even when he cannot see.

Turn to page 3
The servant obeyed the master and did the things he was supposed to do.

The servant said:
I am a faithful servant,
As wise as wise can be.
I do just what my master says
Even when he cannot see.

Turn to page 4
When the master came home, he found the servant hard at work. The master was pleased with the servant.

The servant said:
I am a faithful servant,
As wise as wise can be.
I do just what my master says
Even when he cannot see.

Jesus told this story to help people understand how to obey God. We can obey God even when no one is watching us.

Bible Verse Fun

Choose a child to hold the Bible open to Ephesians 6:1.

Say: Our Bible tells us to obey God and our parents.

> ## We can obey God,
> ## and we can obey our parents.

Say the Bible verse, "Children, obey your parents" (Ephesians 6:1), for the children. Have the children say the Bible verse after you.

Help the children learn the Bible verse by singing. Sing the words printed below to the tune of "God Is So Good."

> "Children, obey.
> Children, obey.
> Children, obey,
> Obey your parents."

Let the children move to the Bible verse. Use a drum or set of rhythm sticks. If you do not have these instruments available, use blocks or unsharpened pencils. Tap two blocks or unsharpened pencils together like you would rhythm sticks. Or pat your hands on the table top or your thighs.

Say the Bible verse, "Children, obey your parents" (Ephesians 6:1), for the children. Beat the instruments on each syllable with a steady beat. Have the children say the verse with you as you beat the instrument.

Then beat the drum and have the children say the verse again without you saying it.

Finally, give each child a drum or set of rhythm sticks (or blocks or unsharpened pencils). Or have the children pat their hands on the table top or their thighs.

Have the children play the beat and say the verse by themselves.

Supplies

Reproducible 12B, water-color markers or watercolor paints and paintbrushes, permenent marker or pen

Promises, Promises

Photocopy the rainbow picture **(Reproducible 12B)** for each child. Let the children decorate the pictures with watercolor markers or with watercolor paints.

Say: Our Bible tells us to obey God and our parents. Today our Bible story is a story Jesus told to help people understand how to obey God.

> **We can obey God, and we can obey our parents.**

Talk with each child as she or he decorates the picture. Have each child tell you one thing he or she will do to obey his or her parents. Write what the child says in the space provided on the picture with a permenent marker or pen. You may need to suggest things to the child such as brush teeth, pick up toys, go to bed on time, and so forth.

Supplies

None

Yes!

Have the children stand in an open area of the room.

Say: Our Bible tells us to obey God and our parents. Let's practice obeying God and our parents.

Say the response verse printed below. Have the children respond as suggested.

Dad tells you to go to bed. To obey, what do you say?
Yes, Dad! *(Shake hands at knee height.)*

Mom asks you to stay in the back yard. To obey, what do you say?
Yes, Mom! *(Shake hands at shoulder height.)*

God wants you to learn from the Bible. To obey, what do you say?
Yes, God! *(Shake hands above head.)*

Yes, Dad! *(Shake hands at knee height.)*
Yes, Mom! *(Shake hands at shoulder height.)*
Yes, God! *(Shake hands above head.)*

© 1994 Cokesbury

Tell Us What to Do

Supplies

None

Have the children sit in a circle on the floor.

Say: When we obey, it means that we do whatever we are told to do. When we obey our parents, we do the things our parents tell us to do.

Ask: What are some things your parents tell you to do? *(brush your teeth, pick up your toys, go to bed, wake up, take a bath, come to supper, wash your hands)*

Say: When we obey God, we do the things God wants us to do.

Ask: What are some things God wants us to do? *(listen to Bible stories, pray, go to church, love others, help others, praise God, be kind, forgive one another)*

Say: Let's practice obeying. Each of you will have a turn to tell us what to do and we will all obey.

Choose a child to move to the middle of the circle. Say the refrain printed below. Have the child tell the remaining children what to do. You may need to give some suggestions such as hop up and down, clap your hands, turn around, say the Bible verse, touch the floor, touch your nose, and so forth. Continue until each child has an opportunity to be in the middle.

(Child's name, child's name)
Tell us what to do.
(Child's name, child's name)
We'll obey you.

Guess Who Prayers

Supplies

None

Have the children sit in a circle on the floor.

Say: I'm thinking of a friend in our circle. Can you guess who?
(Describe one child until the other children guess the child's name.)

Have the child stand up.

Pray: *(Child's name)* **can obey. Thank you, God, for** *(child's name)*. **Amen.**

Continue until you have described each child and yourself.

2. The master gave the servant things to do for him while the master was away.

3. The servant obeyed the master and did the things he was supposed to do.

4. When the master came home, he found the servant hard at work. The master was pleased with the servant.

1. Jesus told a story about a wise servant.

REPRODUCIBLE 12A

I promise to

children, obey your parents.
Ephesians 6:1

REPRODUCIBLE 12B

Responsibility

Bible Verse

Do good to everyone.

Galatians 6:10, GNT

Bible Story

Matthew 25:14–30

Responsibility is a Christian virtue that recognizes and accepts our duty to do God's work each day. Our responsibility as Christians is to build up the kingdom of God.

The parable of the talents is a story of how we are to use what God has given us to further the kingdom of God.

We all have been given abilities and the means with which to further God's kingdom. Some of us have been given the ability to move people with the words we speak; others have been given the ability to cure the sick; and once in a great while we find that one of us has been given the ability to lead a nation closer to God.

Most of us have only seemingly small gifts to give to further God's kingdom, such as the ability to be a Sunday school teacher or collect money for the poor. But in the parable of the talents we see that this does not absolve us of the responsibility of using those small gifts to bring the kingdom of God closer.

Perhaps the man with five talents can be likened to a world leader who had the ability to bring countries together to talk about peace.

Perhaps the person with two talents is like a local pastor with the ability to preach. These people have used their gifts for the furthering of God's kingdom.

Then perhaps the servant with the one talent is like the average person. She or he may not have an impact on an entire church congregation. But if he or she will use that talent, he or she can help increase the kingdom of God proportionately.

Perhaps the Sunday school teacher will influence another world leader, or the person who takes food to the poor will help feed a future pastor. We do not all have the same talents, but we all have the same responsibility.

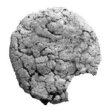

We can be responsible and do good things.

If time is limited, we recommend those activities that are noted in **boldface**. Depending on your time and the number of children, you may be able to include more activities.

ACTIVITY	TIME	SUPPLIES	
Small, Big, Biggest	5 minutes	Reproducible 13A, scissors	**JOIN THE FUN**
Four Corners	**10 minutes**	**Reproducible 13A, scissors, tape**	
Around the Room	5 minutes	None	**BIBLE STORY FUN**
Bible Story: Three Servants	**10 minutes**	**None**	
Bible Verse Fun	**10 minutes**	**Bible, drum, set of rhythm sticks, blocks, or unsharpened pencils.**	
Caught Being Good	10 minutes	Reproducible 13B, crayons or markers, scissors, envelopes, glue	
Responsible Response	5 minutes	None	
Do Good Things	10 minutes	smiley faces (Reproducible 13B), scissors, tape	**LIVE THE FUN**
Guess Who Prayers	**5 minutes**	**None**	

Supplies

Reproducible
13A,
scissors

Small, Big, Biggest

Photocopy and cut out at least two copies of the Bible-times figures **(Reproducible 13A)**. Place the figures on the table. Let the children match the pictures.

Say: **Our Bible tells us to be responsible and to do good things. Today our Bible story is a story Jesus told about a rich man and three servants. Find the rich man in the pictures. Find the servant with the biggest bag of money. Find the servant with the big bag of money. Find the servant with the small bag of money. Jesus told the story to help people understand that God wants us to be responsible and do good things.**

We can be responsible and do good things.

Supplies

Reproducible
13A, scissors,
tape

Four Corners

Photocopy and cut out the Bible-times figures **(Reproducible 13A)**. Show the children each figure.

Say: **Today our Bible story is a story Jesus told about a rich man and three servants.** *(Hold up the picture of the rich man.)* **This is the rich man.** *(Hold up the picture of the servant with the biggest bag of money.)* **This is Servant One. He has the biggest bag of money.** *(Hold up the picture of the servant with the medium-size bag of money.)* **This is Servant Two. He had a big bag of money.** *(Hold up the picture of the servant with the smallest bag of money.)* **This is Servant Three. He has the smallest bag of money.**

Tape one of the pictures in each of the four corners of the room. Have the children move to the center of the room.

Say: **Hop to the rich man.** *(Have all the children hop to the corner that has the picture of the rich man.)* **Now tiptoe to the picture of the servant with the biggest bag of money.** *(Have all the children tiptoe to the corner that has the picture of Servant One.)* **Now crawl to the picture of the servant with the big bag of money.** *(Have all the children crawl to the corner that has the picture of Servant Two.)* **Now fly to the picture of the servant with the small bag of money.** *(Have all the children pretend to fly to the corner that has the picture of Servant Three.)*

Around the Room

Lead the children to your story area with the following movement poem.

Supplies

None

Here we go a-marching,
(March around the room.)
A-marching, a-marching.
Here we go a-marching
all around the room.

Who do we see marching,
(March around the room.)
Marching, marching?
Who do we see marching
All around the room?

We see *(name each child).*
(Stop moving.)

Here we go a-hopping,
(Hop around the room.)
A-hopping, a-hopping.
Here we go a-hopping
all around the room.

Who do we see hopping,
(Hop around the room.)
Hopping, hopping?
Who do we see hopping
All around the room?

We see *(name each child).*
(Stop moving.)

Here we go a-sitting,
(Sit down in your story area.)
A-sitting, a-sitting.
Here we go a-sitting
right here in the room.

Who do we see sitting,
(Sit down in your story area.)
Sitting, sitting?
Who do we see sitting
Right here in the room?

We see *(name each child).*

Three Servants

by Daphna Flegal and LeeDell Stickler

Encourage the children hold up fingers each time you name the servants in the story. Have each child to hold up one finger for Servant One, two fingers for Servant Two, and three fingers for Servant Three.

Once there was a rich man. He had three servants.

**Servant One, Servant One,
Count on him to get things done.**

**Servant Two, Servant Two,
This man knew just what to do.**

**Servant Three, Servant Three,
He was lazy, you will see.**

The rich man had to take a trip. He gave each of his servants money to use while he was gone.

**Servant One, Servant One,
Count on him to get things done.**

**Servant Two, Servant Two,
This man knew just what to do.**

**Servant Three, Servant Three,
He was lazy, you will see.**

Servant One used the money to do good things. Servant One had the BIGGEST bag of money. Servant Two used the money to do good things. Servant two had a BIG bag of money. But Servant Three used the money to do nothing. He had the SMALLEST bag of money. Then the master came home.

**Servant One, Servant One,
Count on him to get things done.**

**Servant Two, Servant Two,
This man knew just what to do.**

**Servant Three, Servant Three,
He was lazy, you will see.**

Servant One gave his master the BIGGEST bag of money. The master was happy. Servant Two gave the master the BIG bag of money. The master was happy. Servant Three gave the master his SMALL bag of money. The master was not happy.

"You lazy servant!" shouted the master. "You did nothing with the money I gave you."

**Servant One, Servant One,
Count on him to get things done.**

**Servant Two, Servant Two,
This man knew just what to do.**

**Servant Three, Servant Three,
He was lazy, you will see.**

Jesus told this story to help people understand that God wants us to be responsible and do good things.

Bible Verse Fun

Choose a child to hold the Bible open to Galatians 6:10.

Say: Our Bible tells us to be responsible and to do good to everyone.

> **We can be responsible and do good things.**

Say the Bible verse, "Do good to everyone" (Galatians 6:10, GNT), for the children. Have the children say the Bible verse after you.

Help the children learn the Bible verse by singing. Sing the words printed below to the tune of "The Farmer in the Dell."

> "Do good to everyone.
> Do good to everyone."
> The Bible tells us how to live.
> "Do good to everyone."

Let the children move to the Bible verse. Use a drum or set of rhythm sticks. If you do not have these instruments available, use blocks or unsharpened pencils. Tap two blocks or unsharpened pencils together like you would rhythm sticks. Or pat your hands on the table top or your thighs.

Say the Bible verse, "Do good to everyone" (Galatians 6:10, GNT), for the children. Beat the instruments on each syllable with a steady beat. Have the children say the verse with you as you beat the instrument.

Then beat the drum and have the children say the verse again without you saying it.

Finally, give each child a drum or set of rhythm sticks (or blocks or unsharpened pencils). Or have the children pat their hands on the table top or their thighs.

Have the children play the beat and say the verse by themselves.

Supplies

Reproducible
13B, crayons
or markers,
scissors,
envelopes,
glue

Caught Being Good

Photocopy and cut apart the smiley faces **(Reproducible 13B)** for each child. Set aside one of the smiley faces for each child and give the child the remaining faces.

Let the children decorate the smiley faces with crayons or markers.

Give each child an envelope. Let the children glue one of the smiley faces on the front of the envelope. Help the children put the remaining smiley faces inside the envelope.

Say: Our Bible tells us to be responsible and to do good to everyone. Take your envelope home to your parents. They will use the smiley faces when they see you doing something good.

We can be responsible and do good things.

Responsible Response

Have the children move to an open area of the room. Teach the children the following response:

Look at me, look at me!
(Crouch down; then stand up with arms over head.)
I have responsibility!
(March in place.)

Say the following statements. Have the children say the response after each statement.

I can remember to feed the dog.
I can help pick up my toys.
I can obey my parents.
I can help take out the trash.
I can water the flowers.
I can tell others about Jesus.
I can do good things.

Do Good Things

Supplies

smiley faces
(Reproducible
13B), scissors,
tape

Have the children move to one side of the room. Stand on the other side of the room from the children.

Call each of the children by name and use the suggestions printed below to tell them how to move across the room to you. Once the child reaches you tape a smiley face **(Reproducible 13B)** onto the child's clothing.

Say: *(Child's name)*, **can do good things.**

(Child's name), **you do good things when you come to church, so hop to me.**
(Child's name), **you do good things when you sing the Bible verse song, so tiptoe to me.**
(Child's name), **you do good things when you share the crayons, so take giant steps to me.**
(Child's name), **you do good things when you listen to the Bible story, so take baby steps to me.**
(Child's name), **you do good things when you wait your turn, so walk backwards to me.**
(Child's name), **you do good things when you put away the toys, so jump to me.**

> ## We can be responsible and do good things.

Guess Who Prayers

Supplies

None

Have the children sit in a circle on the floor.

Say: I'm thinking of a friend in our circle. Can you guess who?
(Describe one child until the other children guess the child's name.)

Have the child stand up.

Pray: *(Child's name)* **can obey. Thank you, God, for** *(child's name)*. **Amen.**

Continue until you have described each child and yourself.

Servant 1

Servant 2

Servant 3

Man

REPRODUCIBLE 13A

REPRODUCIBLE 13B

All-in-One BIBLE FUN

Are you

- Feeling the budget pinch in your children's ministry?
- Unsure of the number of children you'll have in Sunday school each week?
- Working with a Sunday school program that doesn't meet each week?

LET THE FUN BEGIN

Order Today!

Preschool

Elementary

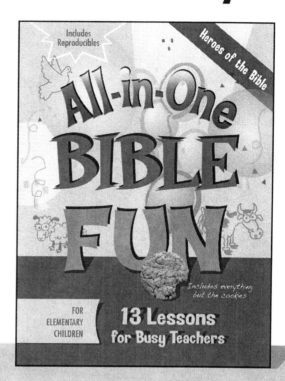

All-in-One Bible Fun

is available for preschool and
elementary-age children. Each book
will focus on a specific theme:

- *Stories of Jesus*
- *Favorite Bible Stories*
- *Fruit of the Spirit*
- *Heroes of the Bible*

- Thirteen complete lessons in each book

- No additional components to purchase

- Each book includes lesson plans with
  your choice of arrival activities, a Bible
  story, a Bible verse and prayer, and games
  and crafts

- Material is undated so teachers can use
  the books throughout the year

All-in-One Bible Fun: 13 Lessons for Busy Teachers

Stories of Jesus—Preschool 978-1-426-70778-0
Stories of Jesus—Elementary 978-1-426-70779-7

Favorite Bible Stories—Preschool 978-1-426-70783-4
Favorite Bible Stories—Elementary 978-1-426-70780-3

Fruit of the Spirit—Preschool 978-1-426-70785-8
Fruit of the Spirit—Elementary 978-1-426-70782-7

Heroes of the Bible—Preschool 978-1-426-70784-1
Heroes of the Bible—Elementary 978-1-426-70781-0

 **Abingdon Press**

abingdonpress.com | 800-251-3320

One Room SUNDAY SCHOOL.

Working with a broader age group?

One Room Sunday School is designed specifically for a program where four or more age groups are taught in one classroom.

For children age 3 through middle school!

Students will grow together through comprehensive Bible study, application of Bible lessons to everyday discipleship, and a variety of age-appropriate activities.

 **Abingdon Press**

Live B.I.G.'s
One Big Room

A Proven Sunday School Program for Mixed-Age Group Children's Ministries

kit includes everything you need for the quarter

- 3 DVDs
- One Music CD
- One Leader Book

For children age 3 through middle school!

𝄞 **Abingdon Press**

CPSIA information can be obtained at www.ICGtesting.com
Printed in the USA
LVOW020742281211

261342LV00001B/20/P